Wild Tiles

Wild Tiles

Creative mosaic projects for your home

CHRISSIE GRACE

NORTH LIGHT BOOKS
CINCINNATI, OHIO
www.artistsnetwork.com

10 09 08 07 06   5 4 3 2 1

Distributed in Canada by Fraser Direct
100 Armstrong Avenue
Georgetown, ON, Canada L7G 5S4
Tel: (905) 877-4411

Distributed in the U.K. and Europe by David & Charles
Brunel House, Newton Abbot, Devon, TQ12 4PU, England
Tel: (+44) 1626 323200, Fax: (+44) 1626 323319
Email: postmaster@davidandcharles.co.uk

Distributed in Australia by Capricorn Link
P.O. Box 704, S. Windsor, NSW 2756 Australia
Tel: (02) 4577-3555

Library of Congress Cataloging-in-Publication Data
Grace, Chrissie.
 Wild tiles : creative mosaic projects for your home /
Chrissie Grace. -- 1st ed.
     p. cm.
 Includes index.
 ISBN-13: 978-1-58180-908-4 (alk. paper)
 ISBN-10: 1-58180-908-5
 1. Mosaics--Technique. I. Title.
 TT910.G7 2006
 738.5--dc22
                                    2006014756

fw
F+W PUBLICATIONS, INC.

EDITOR: David Oeters
COVER DESIGNER: Marissa Bowers
INTERIOR DESIGNER: Brian Roeth
PRODUCTION COORDINATOR: Greg Nock
PHOTOGRAPHERS: Christine Polomsky, Chrissie Grace and
     Jim Gilmore, OMS Photography Inc.
STYLIST: Laura Robinson

Metric Conversion Chart

TO CONVERT	TO	MULTIPLY BY
Inches	Centimeters	2.54
Centimeters	Inches	0.4
Feet	Centimeters	30.5
Centimeters	Feet	0.03
Yards	Meters	0.9
Meters	Yards	1.1
Sq. Inches	Sq. Centimeters	6.45
Sq. Centimeters	Sq. Inches	0.16
Sq. Feet	Sq. Meters	0.09
Sq. Meters	Sq. Feet	10.8
Sq. Yards	Sq. Meters	0.8
Sq. Meters	Sq. Yards	1.2
Pounds	Kilograms	0.45
Kilograms	Pounds	2.2
Ounces	Grams	28.4
Grams	Ounces	0.04

Dedication

This book is dedicated to my family:

To my husband, Mike, who encourages me to pursue my dreams on a daily basis.

To Carson, who has accepted me with open arms.

To my sons, Logan and Ashton, who provide me with more inspiration and imagination than I ever dreamed possible.

And to our newest addition, Ava, who grew inside of me during every step of this journey.

I love you all so much!

About the Author

Chrissie Grace is a mixed-media mosaic artist. In addition to working on her art full-time, she also teaches elementary school art in the public school system.

Chrissie's work focuses on her dreams and intuitions. It focuses on the expansion of her creativity and always testing her limits. It is her hope and mission that her artwork will inspire others. Her work is colorful and full of texture and substance, as well as inspiring themes.

Chrissie lives and works in Orlando, Florida, with her lovely family. To learn more about Chrissie and her mixed-media mosaic artwork, visit her Web site at www.wildtilesmosaics.net.

Acknowledgments

First, I would like to thank Tricia Waddell and North Light Books for believing in me as a first-time author. Also, I would like to thank my editor, David Oeters, for his patience, enduring enthusiasm and constant reassurance. Lastly, thanks to photographer Christine Polomsky and designer Brian Roeth for bringing my images to life.

Thank you all!

Table of Contents

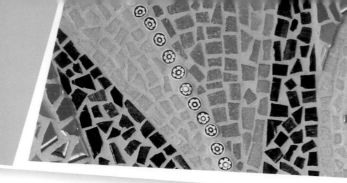

Wild Tiles 9

Getting Started 10
Materials 10
Surfaces 11
Tools and Supplies 12

Techniques 14
Nipping Tile 14
Scoring Glass 15
Using a Jigsaw 16
Using Grout 17

Whimsical Beginnings 18

Wine Bottle Candleholders 20
A Chorus of Light 23

The Night Cat 24
Whooo Are You? 27

Swirls and Glass 28

Eclectic Clutch 32

Eccentric Reflections 36

Do You See What I See? 38
Sea Yourself 41

You Are My Sunshine 42
A Creative Concoction 45

Textured Tiles 46

Majestic Roses 50
Seeds of Sunshine 53

Golden Visions 54

Poignant Projects 58

Bloom 60
Music Heals the Soul 63

Truth Is Universal 64
Perfect Balance 67

Sentimental Elements 68

Magical Memories 72
Words to Live By 75

Bold and Brave 76

Forbidden Fruit 78
More Than a Tree 81

Mystical Mermaid 82
The Coy Geisha 87

Glimpse into Mother Earth 88
The Rainbow River 91

Taking It to the Extreme 92

Birds of Paradise 94
Celestial Wishes 97

Rainy Days 98
Radical Robot 101

The Queen Bee 102

Fairy Amour 108
She Danced until the Sun Came Up 113

Patterns 114

Resources 126

Index 127

"you yourself are a mosaic, shattered,

fragmented, and awesome to behold."

— ANONYMOUS

Wild Tiles

I find a lot of truth inside that quote.

After studying and dabbling in drawing, painting, sculpture, ceramics, quilting, collage, photography, fiber art, glassblowing and bead work, I finally found my niche in mosaics. Eight years ago, I took a local class on mosaics where I made a planter pot. I was hooked instantly; hooked on the freedom of mosaic art and the eternal possibilities it holds.

There is something calming and therapeutic about assembling a mosaic. As the quote says: You are putting the pieces together, just like we do in life. We all have different life experiences—some good, some bad, some beautiful, some not—and all those experiences make up who we are. Mosaics are the same way: Many different pieces make up the mosaic. You take all those shattered and fragmented pieces, those wild tiles, and put them together to create something unique and awesome. The destiny of a mosaic lies in your hands, the hands of the artist.

It is my hope that you see the whimsy, magic and possibility in your life and transfer it to your artwork. Please don't be afraid to get your hands dirty and delve into the opportunities you have created by trying the projects in this book. Most of all, have fun!

Chrissie Grace

Getting Started

Materials

Making a fabulous mosaic is easier than you might think.

The truth is, a beautiful mosaic starts with beautiful materials. The materials used to make a mosaic are known as *tesserae*. At one time, the word tesserae specifically referred to small squares of stone or tile used in making a mosaic, but today it refers to any material you could think of to use in creating mosaic artwork. We mosaic-makers are fortunate today because there is a wider variety of beautiful tile, glass and stone available for use in mosaics than ever before, and modern adhesives and crafting supplies have further expanded our artistic options.

Ceramic tile ✳ Ceramic tile is inexpensive and easy to find and use. It comes in a range of colors, sizes and patterns, and can be found in many places, from home improvement stores to online shops. Tiles can be broken with a hammer or nippers, or cut with a wet saw. Most ceramic tiles are unsuitable for cold-weather outdoor projects, as they are usually not frost-proof.

Smalti ✳ Smalti are the classic mosaic material, first used by Byzantine craftsmen. Small, thick chunks of handmade rectangular glass, smalti are available in an array of beautiful colors. It is particularly useful when creating mosaic portraits. However, it can be expensive and is usually not grouted.

Vitreous glass ✳ Vitreous glass is versatile and easy to cut, and can be used on both indoor and outdoor projects. It is manufactured in regular squares that have smooth tops and rippled bottoms for easy adhesion. Vitreous glass comes in an assortment of colors, and is often mixed with a metallic powder to give it a beautiful shimmer.

Crockery ✳ Crockery is one of my favorite mosaic materials. This term refers to broken pieces of china, mugs, cups, odd plates and bowls that can be used in your mosaics. Crockery presents endless possibilities of colors, patterns and textures. It can be either recycled from your own home or picked up inexpensively at garage sales, flea markets and thrift stores.

Mixed-media elements ✳ Collecting objects such as buttons, beads, shells, stained glass pieces, jewelry, mirrors and game pieces is a fun way to add personality and whimsy to your mosaics. Anything that can be glued down can be used in mosaics; just be sure to pay special attention to fragile pieces when gluing and grouting.

Paper ✳ Paper may not be your first choice for mosaics, but it is extremely accessible and requires little safety attention. Look for handmade papers, scrapbook papers, wallpaper, gift wrap and construction paper. Paper mosaics do not work well in functional areas (such as floors, walls and outdoors), and are better used for decoration.

Polymer clay ✳ Polymer clay, a modeling material, is available in a huge assortment of colors and is extremely versatile; you can sculpt it into any number of shapes and textures. Best used as a decorative element, polymer clay requires preparation in a small conventional oven. Follow the manufacturer's instructions that come with the polymer clay for preparation, safety and use.

tip

LET YOUR FRIENDS AND FAMILY KNOW that you are becoming a mosaic artist. They can save broken dishes for you, and keep their eyes out for fantastic and unique finds. Some of my best tesserae are finds that my loved ones spotted or saved for me.

tip YOU HAVE SEVERAL OPTIONS for transferring a pattern to a surface. Sometimes it is easiest to draw freehand right onto the surface. Other times, it is better to use graphite paper. With graphite paper beneath the pattern, trace the pattern with a pencil and the pattern will transfer directly onto the surface. Outline the pattern with a permanent black marker to make it easier to use.

Surfaces

To make a mosaic, you need to have something to hold the tesserae. That's the surface of the mosaic.

With the right adhesive and preparation, almost anything can be used as a surface for a mosaic. A nice, flat surface works best, especially one that holds the adhesive and tesserae well. Below are some of the surfaces I used in this book.

Wood ∗ Most of the projects I make in this book use a wood surface. Medium-density fiberboard (MDF) is the wood I prefer. It is inexpensive and versatile. Available in varying thicknesses, MDF has a consistent surface and is easy to cut with a jigsaw. It should always be primed with a 1:4 solution of water and white craft glue, and is not especially suitable for outdoor use. Water-resistant, exterior-quality plywood is more suitable for outdoor mosaics than MDF.

Glass ∗ The interesting shapes of vases and bottles make excellent surfaces for mosaics. The texture and reflective nature of glass is fun to use in mosaics. When using glass as a surface, make sure the adhesive you use

is appropriate for glass. Read the manufacturer's instructions that come with the adhesive for information on preparing the surface.

Furniture ∗ The most reliable furniture bases for mosaics should be sturdy enough to hold the weight of the tesserae and should have simple shapes. Secondhand stores are great places to find old furniture, especially since your mosaic will hide many scratches and other signs of wear and tear. Dressers, tables, chairs, frames, doors and fireplaces work especially well as mosaic surfaces. Sand off any old paint, then prime the surface with a 1:4 solution of white craft glue and water. Repaint any areas of the furniture that your mosaic will not cover.

Other surfaces ∗ There are many other surfaces, not featured in this book, that can be used for mosaics. Tile backer board, stone, cement, walls and floors are just a few. When planning a mosaic, research the surface carefully before starting, and be aware of how it will react with the materials and adhesive you are using.

Tools and Supplies

Having the right tools and supplies is important when creating a mosaic. I suggest gathering your materials together before you begin, so you aren't searching for a missing tool when you want to be creating a mosaic. Below are some tools and supplies I use. Most of these can be found in your home, but for the rest you may need to search at your local craft or home supply store.

Tile nippers ✱ Tile nippers are essential to the mosaic artist. They are used to cut crockery and tiles into shapes. It is worth investing in a good pair of nippers, which are available at home improvement stores as well as mosaic specialty shops. The blades have tungsten-carbide edges, which cut cleanly through glass and tiles.

Glass cutter ✱ Glass cutters have a tiny tungsten-carbide wheel that will score a line in a piece of mirror, glass or stained glass. The glass or mirror can then be gently squeezed on either side of the line for a clean break. Invest in a quality glass cutter that's oil-filled. It will keep the wheel lubricated, which will enable you to make easy score lines.

Hammer ✱ Hammers are useful for breaking thick pieces of tesserae as well as larger objects that need to be scaled down. To keep shards from flying around, place the objects beneath an old towel before breaking them with a hammer. Lift the towel frequently to see how the pieces are breaking.

Safety goggles ✱ Safety goggles are extremely important while cutting tesserae. They protect your eyes from flying shards when nipping or breaking tile.

Tweezers ✱ Tweezers are very handy when laying small tesserae and pushing them into place.

Adhesives ✱ There are many types of adhesives for different kinds of mosaics. Make sure the adhesive you choose will adhere to both the surface and the tesserae you are using, and select one that will dry clear. Always test the adhesive before you begin a project. Brand-name Weldbond tile adhesive is excellent for mosaics. It holds up well, is non-toxic, and is available at various online mosaic supply stores. Other types of adhesive that are designed for mosaics will also work well. Clear silicone sealant can be used to adhere glass to glass or any other surface. It is good for mirrors because it won't eat away at the silver backing. Cement-based adhesive is suitable for work that will be displayed outside. It will adhere most tesserae as well as concrete, stone, wood and terracotta. It is also frost- and waterproof.

Grout ✱ Grout protects, supports and frames the tesserae and enhances the overall look of the piece. For many mosaics it is an important part of the process. There are two types of grout: sanded and unsanded. For all the projects in this book that require the use of grout, I recommend that you use sanded grout, which is available in home improvement and craft supply stores and is economical and easy to use. (Unsanded grout can be used only for grout joints that are ⅛" (3mm) or smaller, because in larger joints this type of grout will crack and can be difficult to smooth.) Grout comes in a small variety of colors, but can be mixed with acrylic paint to create other colors. See page 17 for more information on using grout.

Bucket ✱ A bucket is used for mixing grout. If you don't want to dispose of your bucket after grouting, make sure you clean it outside, as grout can clog your drains. Use a paint stick or plastic utensil to mix the grout.

Gloves ✱ Gloves offer your hands protection from the drying effects of grout and are especially useful when you're trying to fit grout into small notches. I find that surgical gloves work best.

tip

IT IS EASIER TO USE small bottles of adhesive than large ones. Adhesive purchased in a large jug can be used to refill smaller bottles as you work. Apply adhesive directly on the back of the tesserae from the smaller bottles. When working with tiny pieces, pour the adhesive directly onto a disposable plate and use tweezers to dip the tesserae into the adhesive and then onto the surface. You'll have much more control this way.

Mask ✱ Always wear a filter mask when mixing grout to prevent breathing in harmful dust particles.

Painter's tape ✱ Tape off areas of your mosaic you want to protect from grout or paint. Masking tape will also work.

Dustpan and brush ✱ Keep a dustpan and brush around when grouting and creating mosaics. Sharp mosaic shards left on the ground can be dangerous.

Cloths and sponges ✱ Cloths and sponges are useful for cleaning grout from a mosaic. Old towels, baby burping pads or discarded, soft T-shirts can be used to wipe down drying grout. Cut them into small squares for easier use when cleaning and polishing.

Acrylic paints ✱ Grout colorants are available from tile suppliers, but acrylic paints work just as well to color grout. Acrylic paint is inexpensive and is available in a range of colors. The more acrylic paint you use to color grout, the stronger the color will be. Acrylic paint also can be a mixed-media element in a mosaic, and can finish the edges of a mosaic with color.

Sealers ✱ Polyacrylic sealers are water-based, clear-drying sealers that provide good, protective finishes for any porous items, such as shells or wooden game pieces, that you may include in your mosaics. Use the sealer before you grout to further protect these surfaces from the damaging effects of grout. If you use polymer clay in a mosaic, you'll also need a polymer clay sealer. Apply this air-drying glaze with a small brush to protect the clay and give it extra shine.

tip

MAKE SURE YOU CHOOSE the correct adhesive when you plan outdoor projects. Make sure the adhesive suits the surface as well. There is nothing worse than completing a project, only to have it fall apart because you chose the wrong adhesive.

Techniques

Don't be intimidated by the use of new tools and techniques. Mistakes are inevitable, but you'll be amazed at how quickly your skills improve as you practice. Remember, starting and learning anything new takes courage and a sense of adventure.

Nipping Tile

One technique you'll use often in making mosaics is nipping tile. It might seem intimidating at first, using a claw-shaped cutting device on a tile, but it's not hard. Trust me! Practice on cheap white tiles that are available at home improvement stores. Always try to nip over a towel to keep small pieces from bouncing off your work surface.

1 | 2
3 | 4

1 *Make the first cut*

Make your first cut halfway along one side of the tile. Place the edge of the tile just inside the cutting area of the nippers and squeeze firmly. Be prepared for the tile to split in half. Although it may feel awkward and a little uncomfortable at first, it becomes much easier with practice.

2 *Continue cutting*

Continue cutting the tile in half, using the same technique you used when making the first cut.

3 *Aim for the correct size*

Continue until you have the size mosaic pieces you'll need for the project. Once the pieces are small, hold the tile on the sides and nip carefully at a point where you won't cut your fingers.

4 *Shape the tile*

Create a variety of shapes in the tile by nipping at different angles. For more control, score the ceramic tile first, then break the tile gently with your nippers on the line.

Scoring Glass

Scoring glass is another technique that seems harder than it really is. With a good score, glass will break cleanly and easily. Just be safe and careful. Wear safety goggles, and if you worry about cutting yourself on the sharp edges of the glass, wear protective gloves as well.

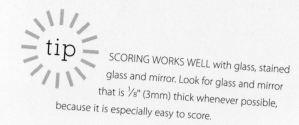

tip SCORING WORKS WELL with glass, stained glass and mirror. Look for glass and mirror that is 1/8" (3mm) thick whenever possible, because it is especially easy to score.

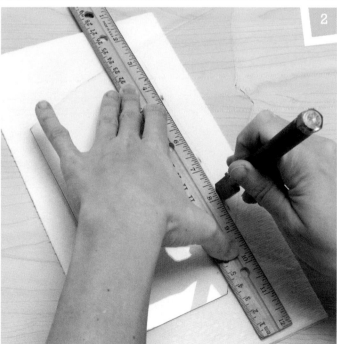

1 *Plan*
Use a pattern and ruler to plan the score lines on the glass.

2 *Score the glass*
Place the glass securely on your work surface. Use a protective cover beneath the glass to make sure the tool doesn't damage your work surface. Using a straight edge, firmly press the scoring tool on the glass and score.

3 *Break the glass*
Holding the glass on either side of the score, make a smooth motion and break the glass on the score.

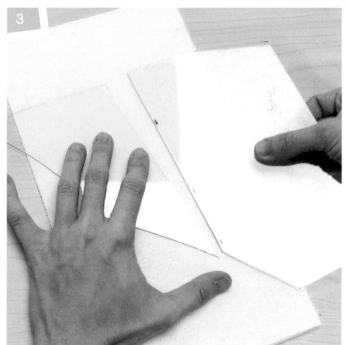

Using a Jigsaw

Don't be intimidated by power tools. They're not hard to use, as long as you are careful and follow safety guidelines. A jigsaw is the best tool for creating shaped surfaces for your mosaics, and learning to use it will really open up the possibilities for your mosaic designs. You can create virtually any shape you want.

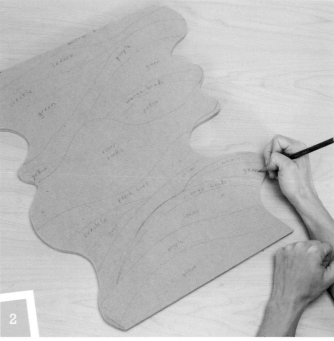

1 *Cut your surface*

Know your equipment before you begin working. Read the instruction manual thoroughly before using any equipment. Keep your jigsaw clean. Maintaining a sharp blade will ensure a reliable cut.

Using a piece of wood no bigger than you'll need, draw the pattern on the wood. Draw only the exterior lines of the pattern, not the interior. Place the wood on a safe work surface, securing it before making your first cut. Keep the wood secure as you cut along the lines, turning the wood as needed. Cut manageable sections of wood away from the pattern.

Always follow the safety guidelines that come with the power tool. Forcing the saw to cut too fast is dangerous. Take your time to avoid damage to your wood and injury to yourself.

2 *Finish your surface preparation*

When you finish cutting, sand the rough edges of the wood, then transfer the interior pattern to the surface.

ALWAYS FOLLOW the manufacturer's instruction on the proper use of a jigsaw—or any power tool. Remember these safety precautions as you work:

* Always wear eye protection and a mask when using a jigsaw. They will protect your eyes and filter out dust particles.
* Make sure to keep loose hair away from power tools. Keep your hair securely bound while working.
* Remove all jewelry, especially loose jewelry, before you begin.
* Secure all loose clothing before you turn on any power tool.
* Be aware of the power cord as you work. Keep it away from water and the work area of the power tool.

Using Grout

Grouting is a useful way to protect and secure your tesserae on the surface, and it can be an important part of a mosaic's design, as well. As previously discussed, I suggest using sanded grout. [Remember that unsanded grout can be used only for mosaics with spaces between tesserae that are $\frac{1}{8}$" (3mm) or smaller. Any larger, and the grout will sink in the space.] To avoid cutting yourself and protect your hands from drying out, wear gloves as you work with grout.

1 Add water

Follow the manufacturer's guidelines to determine the amounts of grout and water needed. Follow the instructions as you mix the grout in a bucket. It is better to slowly add water as you mix than to end up with too much water.

2 Mix the grout

Stir the grout vigorously, adding more grout or water until the mixture reaches a consistency a little thicker than pancake batter.

3 Spread the grout

Lay a large spot of grout on the mosaic, then slowly spread the grout over the surface, making sure it penetrates all the spaces between tesserae. Watch out for sharp edges on the tesserae. Continue adding grout to the surface until all the spaces are filled.

4 Clean away the grout

Once the grout has dried for about ten minutes, begin wiping it away from the surface using an old damp towel or sponge. Be careful that your wiping material is not too wet, so as not to make the grout start spreading again. Be careful not to pull grout from between the tesserae. Once the surface is smooth, buff the tesserae with a clean towel.

"Whatever you can do,
or dream you can, begin it.

Whimsical
Beginnings

Boldness has genius, power and magic in it."

— GOETHE

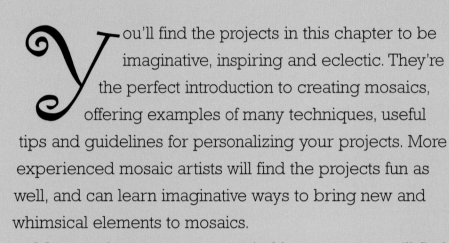

You'll find the projects in this chapter to be imaginative, inspiring and eclectic. They're the perfect introduction to creating mosaics, offering examples of many techniques, useful tips and guidelines for personalizing your projects. More experienced mosaic artists will find the projects fun as well, and can learn imaginative ways to bring new and whimsical elements to mosaics.

Many projects are accompanied by patterns you'll find in the back of the book. Feel free to either use the templates exactly or add and adapt ideas of your own. You might try changing the materials, experimenting with different colors to fit your own style, or using a new pattern. The beauty of mosaic art is its infinite possibilities. Don't hesitate to explore your dreams, find those possibilities, use your own boldness and magic, and really push your creativity! You'll be surprised where it can take you.

Wine Bottle Candleholders

WHAT YOU'LL NEED

* Empty wine bottle
* 4" × 4" (10cm × 10cm) ceramic tiles in orange and purple
* Tapered candles
* Fine-grit sandpaper
* Black permanent marker
* Glass candle bases
* Tile nipper
* Bucket
* Dish soap
* Old towel
* Tile adhesive
* White grout

Imagine this gorgeous candleholder glimmering in the warm glow of the setting summer sun. Beautiful and romantic.

This candleholder was made with tile and a recycled wine bottle. Sometimes a simple project with a simple pattern can be even more striking than a complex one. Here I used simple bands of complementary colors. A long tapered candle placed in the top of the bottle creates a relaxing, warm atmosphere when lit.

This quick and easy project can be finished in no time, but the memories you make with a candle in a romantic setting might last a lifetime.

1 | **2**

3 | **4**

1 *Clean bottle*

Choose a bottle with a size and shape that appeals to you. Soak the bottle in hot soapy water, then peel off the label and rinse. Let the bottle dry thoroughly.

2 *Sand bottle*

Sand the bottle with fine-grit sandpaper to give it a rougher surface for the adhesive and tiles.

3 *Plan design*

Using a permanent ink marker, draw a design on the bottle. For this bottle, I used straight lines of alternating complementary colors.

4 *Nip tiles*

Nip your tiles to form pieces the size of a dime or smaller. Sort the colors into piles.

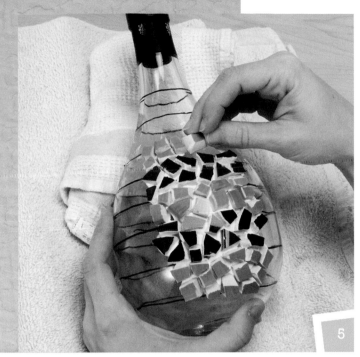
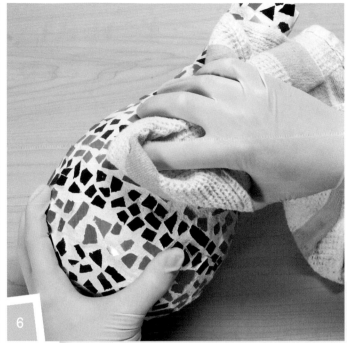

5   6

5 *Lay tile*

Lay the bottle down on an old towel, then apply the tile pieces using adhesive. You will have to work in small sections to keep the tiles from sliding and becoming uneven before the glue dries. After you have finished a section and let the adhesive dry, turn the bottle over on the towel and start a new section. Repeat this process until the mosaic is complete.

6 *Grout*

Let the adhesive dry overnight, then grout the mosaic with white grout, following the instructions on page 17. After the bottle is done, place a tapered candle in the top. Make sure that when you light the candle your bottle is on a glass candle base for safety.

tip

USE DRIP-LESS CANDLES in the bottle to avoid getting wax on the mosaic. Depending on the size of the wine bottle opening, you may have to scrape the bottom of the candles to fit. Always use caution with an open flame, and never leave candles unattended.

A Chorus of Light

The clever use of complementary colors—such as yellow and blue, red and green, or purple and orange—makes it easy to create a series of candleholders. Repeat the steps in the project with each bottle you make.

For more variety, try a swirl or wave pattern on the bottles.

The Night Cat

WHAT YOU'LL NEED

* 13" × 13" (33cm × 33cm) MDF panel
* 4" × 4" (10cm × 10cm) ceramic tiles in black and white
* Found tile or crockery for your cat's "fur" (I used coffee mugs in shades of gold mustard and terra cotta)
* Green tile for grass
* Yellow or gold glass stars and moon
* Two turquoise flat-backed glass marbles
* Acrylic paint in black and turquoise
* Beaded fringe
* Tile nippers
* Black permanent marker
* Paintbrush
* Tweezers
* Painter's tape
* Glue gun
* Craft glue
* Tile adhesive
* White grout
* Pattern (page 114)

Sometimes, even a simple mosaic can take on a life of its own. That's what happened with the Night Cat.

At night, this cat sits and cries to the moon. He is mysterious, inexplicable, superstitious and so attractive to all the female cats. He is mischievous, playful and alluring. Creating this mosaic was just the beginning of an adventure that continues with the stories that are told about the Night Cat. As you work, you may notice your mosaics taking on a life of their own.

I love the turquoise marbles used for the eyes. They create a dramatic effect as the cat seems to come alive. The beaded fringe is an easy way to embellish the project. This mosaic makes an excellent decoration for any room, and is sure to attract attention.

1 2
3 4

1 Prepare surface

Prepare the surface of the wood by mixing a solution of 1:4 craft glue and water. Paint the solution on the surface and let dry. Transfer the cat pattern on page 114 to the MDF board. Go over the lines with a permanent marker to make it easier to see as you work.

2 Begin mosaic

Start by outlining the shape of the cat with white tile. Break the white tiles into small pieces with your tile nippers.

3 Finish cat

Use turquoise glass beads for the eyes of the cat. Outline the cat's nose and mouth with tiny black tiles. Create spots for the cat using terra cotta tile. Fill in the rest of the cat with your gold mustard tiles.

4 Finish background

Fill in the lower background with green tiles, outlining the grass with a lighter green glass. Space the glass stars and moon evenly across the background, then fill the sky with black tiles. Allow the adhesive to dry overnight.

5 6

5 *Grout*

Tape the sides with painter's tape. Mix turquoise acrylic paint and white grout to create a light shade of aqua grout. (See page 17 for more information on grouting.) The grout provides a colorful contrast for the dark-colored tiles. After the piece is dry and the grout has been cleaned, remove the painter's tape and paint the edges with black acrylic paint. Let dry overnight.

6 *Add fringe*

Glue a beaded fringe on the back side of the mosaic, so the beads hang below the mosaic.

tip COFFEE MUGS that are purchased at garage sales or close-out bargain sales can be nipped and used for mosaics. They come in beautiful colors and designs.

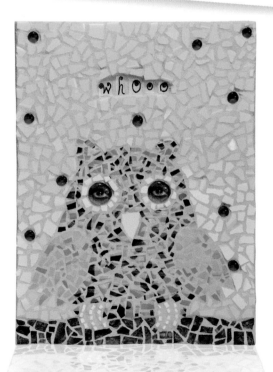

Whooo Are You?

For this variation, I chose an owl, the timeless image of classic wisdom. I made the owl anthropomorphic by gluing images of human eyes under clear, flat-backed glass marbles. This gives the owl a personable yet mysterious demeanor and adds to the wonder of the project. Try to find tile or vintage crockery with an interesting pattern to use for the owl's body.

Swirls and Glass

WHAT YOU'LL NEED

* 4" × 6" (10cm × 15cm) rectangular glass vase
* 20mm (¾" × ¾" × ⅛") square vitreous glass tiles in a variety of shades of green and white
* Small green flat-backed glass marbles
* Pink acrylic paint
* Permanent marker
* Tweezers
* Tile nippers
* Painter's tape
* Cotton swabs
* Tile adhesive
* White grout

Flowers should always be complemented by beautiful vases. That is to say, they should be complemented, but not overwhelmed. The swirls on this modern vase are subtle in their beauty and are meant to accentuate the natural beauty of a spring bouquet. The simple design and use of gorgeous glass are what make this project so striking.

The simple pattern—freehand swirls—adds to the elegance of the glass, rather than making the pattern the focus.

After spending a winter with holiday-themed bouquets, I look forward to the return of spring and the wonderful flowers that come with the season. My favorite flowers to put in this vase are tulips or daisies.

tip WHEN WORKING WITH SMALL TESSERAE, it's a good idea to use tweezers to help position the pieces. Avoid disturbing the tesserae around each piece as much as possible.

1 *Plan design*

Using a black permanent marker, draw a free-form swirl on the front of the vase. Make sure the swirls are large enough to be lined with the small pieces of tesserae.

2 *Lay marbles*

Working on one side at a time, glue the green flat-backed marbles around the swirls. Use tile nippers to cut the green vitreous glass into small pieces. Lay green vitreous glass along the swirl pattern you created in step 1.

3 *Lay background*

Once the swirls are complete, use tile nippers to cut the white vitreous glass into small pieces. Fill the background around the swirls with the white glass. Work first on just the side with the marbles and green glass swirls.

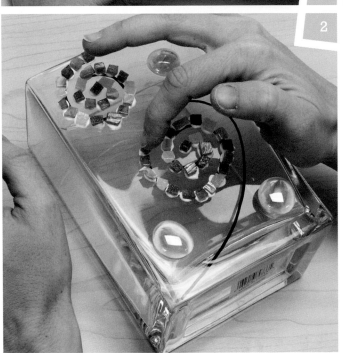

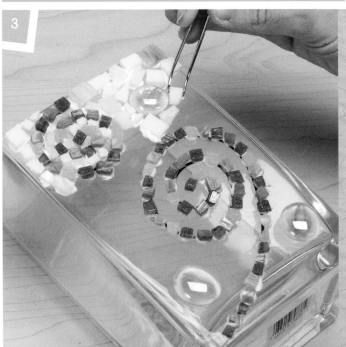

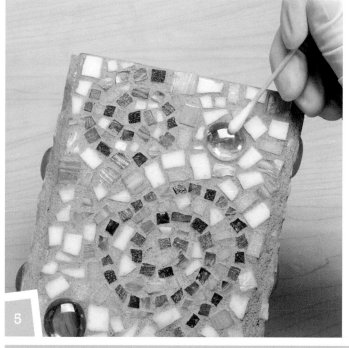

4 5

6

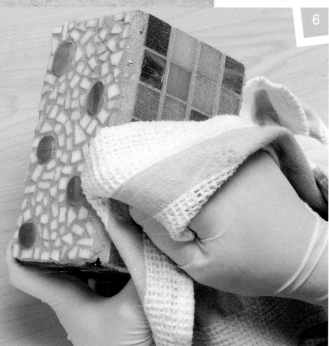

4 *Finish laying tesserae*

Finish laying the background. Make sure that there are no large gaps in the tesserae and that the white glass outlines the swirls. Then, glue more green flat-backed marbles on the two sides of the vase in patterns of your choosing. Add a background of white vitreous glass around them.

5 *Grout*

Tape off the back, bottom and top of the vase. Create pink grout using white grout and pink acrylic paint, then grout the front and sides of the vase with the pink grout. (See page 17 for more on grouting.) Let dry, then carefully clean off the glass. Use a cotton swab to make sure the glass is clean of grout.

6 *Finish vase*

For the back of the vase, lay rows of vitreous tiles. When the adhesive is dry, grout the back of the vase using pink grout.

tip IF YOUR VITREOUS GLASS looks a little cloudy or hazy after the grout has dried, dip a cotton swab into white vinegar. Lightly clean off the glass with the vinegar and it will sparkle.

Eclectic Clutch

WHAT YOU'LL NEED

* Wooden purse base
* Teal acrylic mosaic pieces
* 3/8" (10mm) vitreous glass mosaic tiles in teal, dark brown, gold and moss green
* Five matching, round, flat-backed beads
* Black velvet
* Acrylic paint in green and brown
* Paintbrush
* Small screwdriver
* Scissors
* Cotton swabs
* Polyacrylic sealer
* Painter's tape
* Fabric adhesive
* Tile adhesive
* Tan grout

Mosaics are often used for solely decorative and aesthetic purposes, but I enjoy the challenge of finding functional items that can be the base of a mosaic. This fun project is both functional and creative. You can find many types of wooden purse bases at various arts and crafts stores. I found this one at a local craft store. It is the perfect accessory for carrying essential items.

Most craft stores carry many other functional items made out of wood bases, such as frames, trinket boxes, bird houses and clock bases. Once you are comfortable with the mosaic-making techniques in this book, you could use almost any wood base to design your own functional mosaic project.

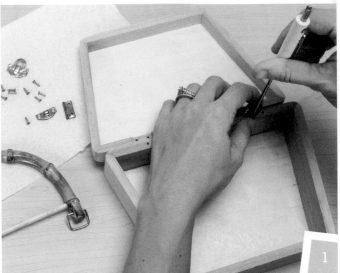

1 *Prepare purse*
Unscrew the latch and handle of the purse, then remove the hinge inside the purse. Save the hardware of the purse for later use.

2 *Lay border*
Lay the front of the purse down flat and glue the vitreous tiles in a pattern around the edge.

3 *Lay beads*
Glue the five beads down. Lay one in the middle, two on top and two on the bottom of the purse front, as shown.

4 *Lay background*
Fill in the background with the teal acrylic mosaic pieces.

tip — AS YOU WORK, make sure you keep your hardware for the purse (any screws, latches, hinges, etc.) in a safe place. If you lose it, you won't be able to reassemble your purse!

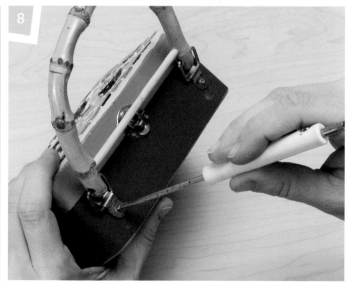

tip FEEL FREE to switch the colors around on this project. Why not try a palette of oranges, reds and purples? If you are making the purse for yourself, look in your closet for the color that dominates your wardrobe, and incorporate that in the mosaic

5 *Paint purse*

Paint the edges of the front top and inside edge with green acrylic paint. Paint the edges of the bottom of the purse with brown, inside and out. Paint the back bottom green. Seal all the acrylic paint with a polyacrylic sealer.

6 *Grout*

When all the paint dries, tape the front edge with blue painter's tape. Grout the front with tan grout. (See page 17 for more information on grouting.) After it dries, clean the grout and remove the tape.

7 *Add felt*

Cut out two pieces of black felt to fit inside the purse. Line the inside front and back with the felt. Use fabric glue to secure the felt inside the purse.

8 *Assemble purse*

Use your screwdriver to put the hinges and handle back on the purse.

"I love mirrors. They let one

Eccentric Reflections

pass through the surface of things."
— CLAUDE CHABROL

All of the projects in this chapter are either mirrors or frames, both of which I find to be very symbolic in nature.

Mirrors are symbols of self-discovery, knowledge of self and contemplation. In many myths, legends and stories, mirrors create gateways or portals, or they serve as important tools in divination. Philosophically, mirrors lead us to question our place in the universe: "Am I looking in, or is someone else looking out?" Whatever the mirror reveals is the truth, as it is an exact reflection of a point in the universe around the user.

Frames are used to enclose things we find precious, aesthetically pleasing or sentimentally valuable. They both protect and embellish, making the objects they frame even better. We often use frames to display pictures of our loved ones.

Philosophically, intellectually, symbolically or however you choose to see these projects, they are gorgeous and fun. Enjoy adding the beauty and wonder of mosaic mirrors and frames to your life. Whatever path has led you to these projects, enjoy the adventure and the treasures you are left with.

Do You See What I See?

Pattern (page 115)

WHAT YOU'LL NEED

* $7^3/_4$" × $7^3/_4$" × $1^1/_4$" (20cm × 20cm × 3cm) wooden frame
* $3^1/_2$" × $3^1/_2$" (9cm × 9cm) mirror
* Ceramic tiles in the following colors: black, white and red
* Two red flat-backed glass marbles
* Fifteen large, clear flat-backed glass marbles
* White and black patterned paper
* Tile nippers
* Paintbrush
* Craft glue
* Tile adhesive
* Silicon adhesive
* Gray grout
* Pattern (page 115)

This little mirror is a mod version of perfect geometric shapes. The black and white tiles accentuate the geometric pattern, while the red tiles throw a little whimsy into the project.

There is something fascinating about mirrors—the reflective quality, the dance of perceived images and the play of light. Mirrors should always be framed in a beautiful or interesting way—and, of course, this mosaic makes the perfect frame.

I took a little inspiration from art giant Andy Warhol to create this mirror. Warhol's work was often geometric in nature, using many black-and-white images. His work was a highlight of Pop Art, which reached its full popularity in New York in the 1960s.

1	2
3	4

1 *Prepare surface*

Prepare the surface of the frame by mixing a 1:4 solution of craft glue and water. Apply the solution with a paintbrush. When dry, transfer the pattern on page 115 to the wooden frame.

2 *Prepare marbles*

Glue the large flat-backed marbles on the patterned paper using craft glue. When dry, cut out the marbles with the paper glued on the back. The pattern should appear through the marbles.

3 *Nip tile*

Using the tile nippers, break the red, black and white tiles into tiny pieces.

4 *Begin mosaic*

Glue the red beads down first, placing one at the middle top and one at the middle bottom. Start filling in the pattern by gluing one geometric box in at a time, using the red, black and white tiles to create the geometric pattern.

5 6

5 *Grout*

Finish by gluing the marbles with the pattern paper along the sides of the frame, making sure the glue has set enough that the beads won't slide off. Let the frame dry overnight, then grout the frame with a gray grout. Clean the grout once it has set. (See page 17 for more information on grouting.)

6 *Add mirror*

After the grout is dry, secure the mirror with silicone adhesive. Let the adhesive dry overnight. Then, use the hardware supplied with the mirror to hang it.

Sea Yourself

This is a much larger mirror, approximately 24" × 24" (61cm × 61cm). The geometric pattern is easy to transfer to any size. When working on the four corners of the project, paint the circle with acrylic paint. Tape off the painted circles before grouting. After you've finished grouting, use adhesive to glue real seashells in the circles.

You Are My Sunshine

WHAT YOU'LL NEED

* 12" × 12" (30cm × 30cm) wooden frame
* Mix of tiny tiles in shades of yellow
* Yellow cobbles (transparent yellow glass shards)
* Tile or crockery in an orange-yellow tone
* Two types of crockery with a yellow theme
* Four small yellow flat-backed glass marbles
* Small clear flat-backed glass marbles
* Acrylic paint in yellow and aqua
* Paintbrush
* Pencil
* Ruler
* Tile nippers
* Computer with printer
* Painter's tape
* Craft glue
* Tile adhesive
* White grout

I took my inspiration for the color palette of this frame from the sun—different shades of yellow, white and gold. The turquoise grout complements the yellow tiles. A variety of tesserae, such as crockery and flat-backed marbles, was used to make a mosaic with texture. This creates a bright, happy frame with plenty of visual interest.

What does it all mean? A mosaic frame this cheerful is perfect for a picture of your sweetheart or someone else you hold dear to your heart. I love to use a black-and-white photo in this frame. It really makes the colors of the frame come alive and elevates the picture to art, just as it should be.

I chose to put a black-and-white photo of my husband and I on our wedding day in this frame. It celebrates the day we united as a couple, and lets him know that he is "my sunshine."

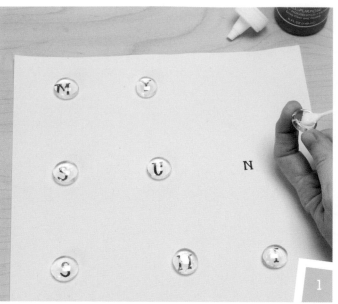

1 *Prepare marbles*

Using your computer's word processor, type the words *My Sunshine* in the font of your choice, leaving plenty of space between the letters. Print the words on white paper. Spread a tiny drop of white craft glue evenly on the back of each marble, and place one marble on each letter. After the glue dries, cut out the marbles. The letters should show clearly beneath the glass.

2 *Begin mosaic*

Prepare the surface of the wood by painting it with a 1:4 solution of craft glue and water. Plan the mosaic layers next. The letters should be beside the picture; then plan successive layers of mosaics around the frame, using a ruler to keep the layers even. Lay a border on the outside edge of the frame with the tiny tiles. Next, place your yellow glass marbles on the frame. Use a tile nipper to cut crockery pieces to fill in another section of the frame, working around the glass marbles.

3 *Continue mosaic*

Using the yellow-orange tesserae to fill another section, continue to cover the frame. Use yellow-themed crockery next. Continue filling sections of the frame with a variety of tesserae.

4 *Finish mosaic*

Finally, once you reach the area just below the picture, glue your letter beads down. Finish filling the area below the beads with the yellow cobbles. Let the adhesive dry overnight.

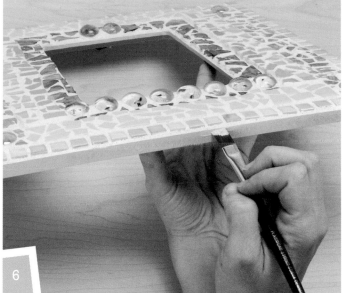

5   6

5 *Grout*
Cover the edges of the frame with painter's tape. Mix aqua acrylic paint in white grout, then grout the frame. (See page 17 for more information on grouting.) After the grout has dried, remove the tape and clean the grout from the tile.

6 *Paint frame*
Paint the inside and outside edges of the frame with yellow acrylic paint. When the paint has dried, place a picture in the frame.

A Creative Concoction

Pique assiette, a French term that means "stolen from the plate," is a fascinating form of folk art. *Pique assiette* was very popular from Victorian times into the early twentieth century, and has been used for garden accessories, furniture and even Simon Rodia's famous Watts Towers in California.

This mirror was finished in the style of *pique assiette* by incorporating pieces of broken ceramics—plates, dishes, cups, tiles and other found objects—in the design. It can be seen as a collage of prepared and found objects, and the variety of designs and patterns combine in unexpected ways. Frames are a fun and wild way to use *pique assiette*.

Textured Tiles

WHAT YOU'LL NEED

* 9" × 7" (23cm × 18cm) frame with a 4" × 6" (10cm × 15cm) opening (Note: The template has the photo on the right side of the frame. The pattern may need to be adjusted for the frame you choose.)

* Two blocks of white polymer clay

* Acrylic paints in the following colors: yellow, ochre, orange-yellow, orange, burnt orange, light blue, turquoise and gold

* Metallic rub-ons

* Variety of stamps (Rubber Stampede)

* Pasta machine or polymer clay roller

* Craft knife

* Carbon paper

* Pencil

* Scissors

* Large ceramic baking tile

* Paintbrush

* Toaster oven

* White gesso

* Polymer clay sealer

* Paper towels

* White craft glue

* Pattern (page 115)

I'm always looking for new mediums to use in mosaics, and new ways to create visual interest and appeal in my work. Polymer clay is a wonderful way to add both.

Polymer clay is a very different medium from tile or glass because it gives you the freedom to create different shapes, colors and textures. I love to use texture in mosaics. Even better, there's no grout involved when you make a mosaic with polymer clay.

I made these textured tiles using stamps, which create the wealth of texture in the clay and are another of my favorite mixed-media items. The frame is meant to look aged, and the black-and-white photo helps enhance the weathered look.

tip ONE OF THE ADVANTAGES of working with polymer clay is that mistakes are easy to fix. Before the clay is baked, you can squish up mussed stamps and start over. Simple!

1   2

3   4

1 Prepare frame

Paint your frame with a coat of gesso. After it dries thoroughly, apply two even coats with a gold acrylic paint. (This background will act as your "grout," since you shouldn't grout polymer clay mosaics.) Copy the template from page 115 directly onto the frame. This will act as your guide to filling in your polymer clay pieces.

2 Prepare clay

Condition your polymer clay by running it through a pasta machine. You can use a polymer clay roller, but using a pasta machine will keep all the pieces level. Use the template and a craft knife to cut out the shapes that will fill your picture frame template.

3 Stamp clay

After you cut out each piece, carefully press a stamp into each piece of clay. The stamp does not need to fit the piece perfectly, but it should cover the clay with a design. The more relief you press into the clay, the more noticeable the design will be.

4 Assemble tiles

Bake the clay on a ceramic tile in a toaster oven preheated to 275°F (135°C) for 30 minutes. Let the clay cool before removing it from the tile. When cool, assemble the tiles on the pattern. If necessary, carefully trim the clay using a craft knife till you're sure the clay will fit nicely in the pattern.

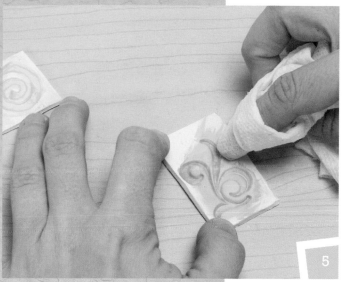

5   6

7

5 *Paint tiles*
Choose a color for each of the mosaic tiles, then paint each tile. Use a paper towel to rub off the paint. The paint will have settled into the stamp design. Do this for each of the tiles.

6 *Embellish tiles*
Embellish the tiles using metallic rub-ons to color the background. After you have finished all the tiles, let them dry, then seal them with a polymer clay sealer.

7 *Finish frame*
Arrange the polymer clay tiles on the frame and use craft glue to secure them in place. Add a picture to the frame to finish.

tip   FOR A BRIGHTER FRAME, use a variety of polymer clay colors to make your tiles. Polymer clay is available in a huge variety of colors! After stamping and baking your tiles, you could still add metallic rub-ons for an interesting look and texture.

Majestic Roses

WHAT YOU'LL NEED

* Rectangular frame measuring 24" × 16" (61cm × 41cm) with an opening measuring 7½" × 11½" (19cm × 29cm)

* Mirror measuring 8" × 12" (20cm × 30cm)

* Mosaic tesserae roses from plates, cups, bowls, vases, etc. Try to collect a nice variety of roses in different colors, shapes and sizes.

* Acrylic paint in red and lavender

* Hammer

* Old towel

* Tile nippers

* Cotton-tipped swabs

* Paintbrush

* Painter's tape

* Craft glue

* Tile adhesive

* Silicone adhesive

* White grout

I am constantly searching for anything with roses on it: plates, cups, ceramic vases, jewelry boxes and more. Anything with a rose on it that can be glued down and grouted is fair game! I search garage sales, thrift stores, estate events and the Internet for tesserae rose treasures.

One glance in this gorgeously feminine and majestic mirror can make anyone feel more beautiful. This mirror makes a great addition to any room that is just calling for fresh roses!

If you would like to add special meaning to your rose mirror, keep these symbolic notions in mind:

* Red roses say "I love you" and also stand for respect and courage.

* Yellow roses represent joy and gladness, and they are also a sign of friendship.

* White roses can have several meanings: reverence and humility, innocence and purity, and perhaps silence.

* Coral or orange roses represent enthusiasm and desire.

* Pink roses also have several meanings: grace and gentility, gratitude and appreciation, or admiration and sympathy.

tip I BOUGHT THIS FRAME AND MIRROR pre-made, but you can make one using a jigsaw (see page 16 for information on using a jigsaw).

1 *Gather material*

Gather rose-themed materials, such as plates, cups and tiles. Nip and break the materials to smaller sizes to fit into a mosaic and to highlight the roses in the design.

2 *Begin mosaic*

Prepare the surface of the frame by painting it with a 1:4 solution of craft glue and water. When dry, begin the mosaic. With the assortment of roses you have collected, your frame is sure to be one of a kind. Try to place a variety of elements together, keeping the assortment random.

3 *Assemble elements*

Highlight design elements as you assemble the mosaic. For example, a big red rose next to a tiny yellow rose makes for a more interesting design, with the smaller element enhancing the larger focal point.

4 *Finish mosaic*

When you finish laying the tesserae, make sure there are no gaps in the design. After the adhesive dries, tape the edges with painter's tape.

5 | 6

7

5 *Mix grout*

Mix the grout, adding the lavender acrylic paint slowly, until you are pleased with the color.

6 *Grout*

Apply the grout carefully to the mosaic, making sure it fills all the empty areas around the dimensional elements on the frame. Once dry, clean the grout from the frame. As you clean the grout, keep cotton-tips handy to clean in the little cracks and crevices of the dimensional ceramic roses.

7 *Paint frame*

Once the grout has set, paint the edges of the frame red. Let the paint dry, then secure the mirror in the frame with silicone adhesive.

Seeds of Sunshine

Take a look in any garden or greenhouse for inspiration for variations on this project. Why not try lilies, African violets or daisies? I used sunflowers to decorate this mirror. I collected as many ceramic versions of sunflowers as I could find. This variation is much smaller than the rose-themed mirror, and works great on a patio or in a kitchen that is decorated with a country theme.

Golden Visions

WHAT YOU'LL NEED

* 24" × 16" (61cm × 41cm) oval wooden frame
* 8" × 12" (20cm × 30cm) mirror
* Vitreous glass in browns, purples, lime green and hot pink
* 1/8" (3mm) clear glass
* Gold tiles
* Flat-backed glass marbles in various colors
* Small, clear flat-backed glass marbles
* Purple acrylic paint
* White paper or cardstock
* Gold ink pen
* Black permanent marker
* Scissors
* Tile nippers
* Glass cutter
* Paintbrush
* Painter's tape
* Craft glue
* Tile adhesive
* Silicone adhesive
* Beige grout
* Pattern (page 116)

Artists are always looking for new inspiration for their work, and mosaic artists are no different. Gustav Klimt's artwork has always held a special appeal for me. His style includes the extensive use of gold Mycenaean-inspired scroll decorations and mosaics. The use of bright colors, two-dimensional patterns, and various circular shapes are other traits of his work. These characteristics can be seen in his most famous painting, *The Kiss*.

I call this my "Klimt" mirror, as it was inspired by my love for Klimt's use of swirls, abstract designs and color. This mirror sparkles with gold tiles and brightly colored vitreous glass. For me it represents the subtle eroticism and glamour that I admire in Klimt's work.

This project calls for handmade tesserae. Paint and markers will create unique designs on paper, and flat-backed marbles will give the design dimension.

1 Prepare frame

Prepare the surface of the frame by mixing a 1:4 solution of craft glue and water. Apply the solution with a paintbrush. Once dry, use the pattern on page 116 to draw the design directly on the wooden frame. Decide what elements you'll be using to fill the design, and plan the frame.

2 Create tesserae

Paint a white piece of paper lavender, and another with purple. Draw designs such as triangles, squares and circles using a black permanent marker on the painted paper, then outline the design in gold. You should make about 40 of these designs, with each design about ⅛" (3mm) wide.

3 Assemble tesserae

Using clear craft glue, glue a clear flat-backed marble over each of the circle designs, then score square, circular and triangular pieces of clear glass to glue over their corresponding designs. Adhere the glass so it fits neatly over the designs. Cut the tesserae from the paper, leaving the designs to show through the pieces of glass. (See page 15 for more information on scoring glass.)

4 Begin mosaic

Begin applying the vitreous tiles to the surface using tile adhesive, working in small sections. Start with the outside lines of each section, nipping the tiles as you go. Work with one color at a time inside each section. Add glass marbles where indicated in the pattern.

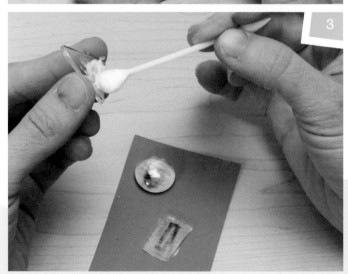

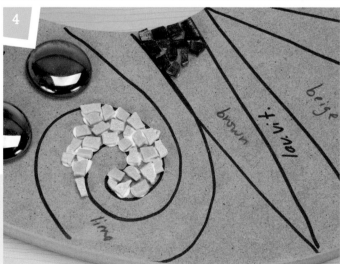

tip IF YOU CAN'T BUY THE FRAME AND MIRROR pre-made, you can make one using a jigsaw on a piece of flat wood. See page 16 for more information on using a jigsaw.

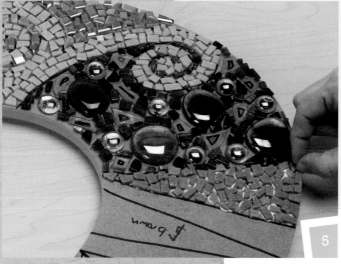

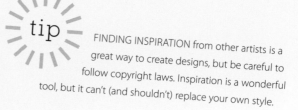

tip FINDING INSPIRATION from other artists is a great way to create designs, but be careful to follow copyright laws. Inspiration is a wonderful tool, but it can't (and shouldn't) replace your own style.

5

6

7

8

5 *Add tesserae*

Add the glass pieces featuring the black and gold designs to some sections first, before filling in the background with the other elements you have planned for those sections. It will be easier to add the designed glass pieces to larger sections in the pattern so that there is enough room for the elements to frame the designed glass pieces.

6 *Finish mosaic*

Finish the design, making sure the mosaic is filled and there are no gaps.

7 *Grout*

Tape the sides of the frame with painter's tape, then grout using beige grout. Be sure to push the grout down in all of the spaces between tesserae. Clean the frame once the grout has dried. After the frame is dry, remove the painter's tape and paint the edges with purple acrylic paint.

8 *Secure mirror*

Secure the mirror to the frame using silicone adhesive. Let the adhesive dry overnight before using the mirror.

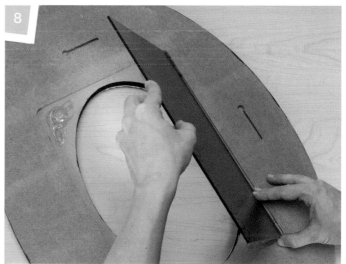

"I know nothing with any certainty,

Poignant
Projects

This chapter's four projects focus on inspiration. What inspires you? What makes you happy? What makes you sad? What makes you nostalgic or hopeful for the future? I believe good art is always inspired by something.

I am frequently inspired by people—my family, friends, my children and strangers I see on the street. Music speaks to me emotionally. Poetry, quotes and books continually inspire. Other artists—their work and outlooks on life—are also inspiring. Inspiration can be found in nature as well—a beach, the mountains, a sunrise, stars, and even objects such as seashells and leaves. Travel inspires me. I love seeing new places, experiencing new cultures, tasting new foods and meeting new people. Even little every-day things, like a good television show or movie, can become creative inspiration.

I encourage you to keep an inspirational journal or folder for future projects. Use it to store creativity-inspiring photos you've taken, poems you've read, pictures you've found in magazines—anything that provokes an idea for a future mosaic. Who knows where you'll find inspiration next?

Bloom

WHAT YOU'LL NEED

* 12" × 18" (30cm × 46cm) piece of MDF

* Polymer clay in the following colors:
  light pink, hot pink, red, lavender,
  orange, yellow, green, white and black

* Game pieces, beads or plastic letters
  spelling out the word BLOOM

* Beige acrylic paint

* Pasta machine or polymer clay roller

* Craft knife

* Flower polymer clay cutter

* Small circle polymer clay cutter

* Large ceramic baking tile

* Paintbrush

* White gesso

* Polymer clay sealer

* White craft glue

* Pattern (page 117)

I like to take realistic objects and give them a simple, abstract twist. This vase of flowers is filled with simple shapes and bright, bold colors. I'm always inspired by the beauty of Mother Nature, and flowers are some of my favorite subjects.

When I first drew the design for this mosaic, I immediately thought to use polymer clay. Besides its pliability, which gives you a sense of freedom that other tesserae cannot, it's also available in an incredible selection of colors. You can also mix together different shades of the clay to create your own unique colors and patterns. If you would like to learn other techniques for using this medium, a quick search of your local arts and crafts store or bookstore will uncover many wonderful books about polymer clay.

1 Prepare surface
Paint the wood with a coat of gesso. After it dries thoroughly, apply two even coats of beige acrylic paint. Make sure you paint the edges of the wood as well. This background will act as your "grout," since you shouldn't grout polymer clay mosaics. Transfer the pattern on page 117 to the wood.

2 Prepare flowers
Condition your polymer clay by running it through a pasta machine. You can use a polymer clay roller, but using a pasta machine will keep all the pieces level. Use your flower cutter to cut out the various flowers, following the pattern. Cut 12 small circles out of the yellow clay for the centers of the flowers.

3 Create vase
Using the pattern as a template for the vase, cut out the whole shape in black polymer clay. Using a craft knife, cut vertical lines to create long tiles in the shape of the vase. Cut out a variety of different-sized triangles from white polymer clay for the background, making sure there are enough triangles to fill the background. Cook the polymer clay on a ceramic tile in a toaster oven at 275°F (135°C) for 30 minutes. Let the clay cool before taking it out of the oven.

4 Assemble mosaic
Seal the baked clay with a polymer clay sealer. Glue the vase down first, following the pattern, then the flowers and the letters. Paint the inside of the vase white.

5 6

5 *Create stems*

Roll out green clay for the stems, and fit the stems on the flowers, trimming, arranging and adding clay as needed. Remove the stems and cook them on a ceramic tile in the oven at 275°F (135°C) for 15 minutes.

6 *Assemble background*

When cool, glue the stems in place. Finally, arrange and glue the white triangle background in place.

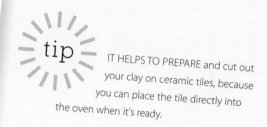

tip IT HELPS TO PREPARE and cut out your clay on ceramic tiles, because you can place the tile directly into the oven when it's ready.

Music Heals the Soul

Like polymer clay mosaics, paper mosaics offer many options. You can use a variety of colors, as well as handmade papers, origami papers or papers that you have stamped, painted or collaged on.

In this variation I used papers I found at my local scrapbook store, as well as white paper I painted using acrylic paints. I drew the image and then cut the paper out in various shapes and started filling in the pieces of the mosaic. I used a thin paintbrush to outline the girl and the piano with black paint to make them stand out.

Don't hesitate to explore the possibilities of paper mosaics on your own!

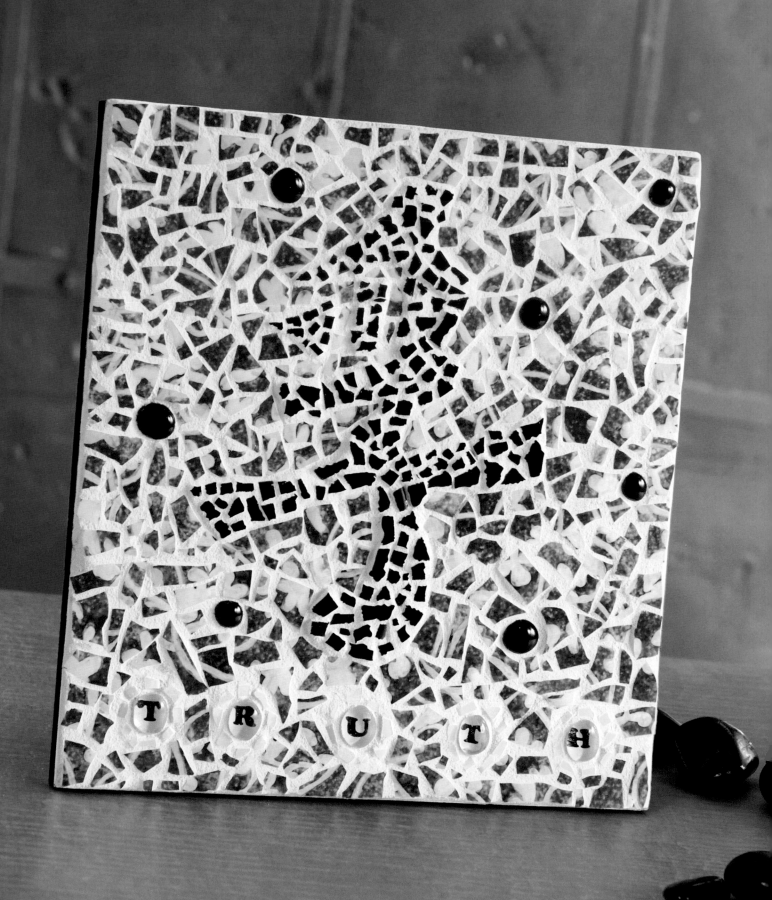

Truth Is Universal

WHAT YOU'LL NEED

* 12" × 12" (30cm × 30cm) piece of MDF
* 4" × 4" (10cm × 10cm) black ceramic tiles
* Assorted crockery with an Asian theme
* 4" × 4" (10cm × 10cm) ceramic tile in yellow (or a color that matches the Asian-themed crockery)
* Large, clear, flat-backed glass marbles
* Black acrylic paint
* Computer and printer
* Tile nippers
* Paintbrush
* Painter's tape
* Craft glue
* Tile adhesive
* White grout
* Pattern (page 118)

The practice of writing

Chinese characters is a form of fine art with more than two thousand years of history behind it. Each symbol is an entire word filled with subtle meaning. I've always felt power in Chinese symbols—from the way they are used in tattoos to the myths and rumors of their magic and power. They seem more like artwork than writing, making them the perfect subject for a mosaic. The aesthetics make them undeniably appealing!

This mosaic of the Chinese character for *truth* is meant to be used as a wall decoration. The choices of tile and colors make the character the focal point of the mosaic. Look for other Chinese characters to create a whole series of mosaics for an Asian-themed room.

1 Prepare letters

Using your computer's word processor, type the word *TRUTH* in a font that will match your design, leaving plenty of space between the letters. Print the word on a white piece of paper. Spread a small amount of white craft glue on the back of clear flat-backed glass marbles, and glue one to each of the separate letters. When dry, cut out the round marbles from the paper with the letters underneath.

2 Prepare surface

Prepare the surface of the wood with a solution of white craft glue and water (1:4). Transfer the pattern on page 118 to the wood. Center the letters underneath the Chinese symbol and use tile adhesive to glue them in place. Add black flat-backed marbles randomly to the background.

3 Lay symbol

Cut the black tile into tiny pieces using tile nippers. Use tile adhesive and black tile tesserae to fill in the Chinese symbol.

4 Finish background

Surround the glass-bead letters with yellow-tile tesserae. This will help the letters stand out from the background. Fill in the rest of the background with colorful Asian-themed crockery tesserae. Allow the mosaic to dry overnight.

5 6

5 *Grout*

Tape the sides of the mosaic with painter's tape. Grout the piece using a white grout. When dry, clean the mosaic throroughly.

6 *Paint*

When the grout has set, remove the painter's tape and paint the edges black.

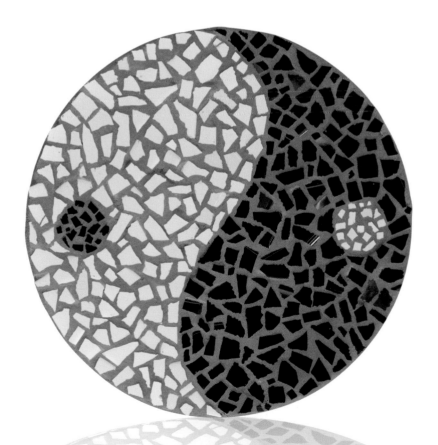

Perfect Balance

Yin and yang are opposites. Yin represents the feminine, eternity and dark and is associated with the moon. Yang is its opposite: masculine, focused on history and light and represented by the sun. According to ancient Chinese philosophers, in the beginning was the Tao. Then the Tao separated into the two prime principles, yin and yang.

I am a firm believer that everything in life is in balance. Everything has a positive and negative, a light and a dark, a left and a right. This variation project represents this truth. It is a simple pattern, but powerful.

FAMILY

Sentimental Elements

WHAT YOU'LL NEED

* 9" × 12" (23cm × 30cm) shadowbox frame
* 9" × 12" (23cm × 30cm) matboard
* Four 3" × 4" (8cm × 10cm) pieces of matboard
* Family photographs that have been scanned from the originals
* Five to six eggs
* White cardstock
* Paints and inks (various colors—I prefer Jacquard inks for this project because of their brilliant colors)
* Stamps or stencils
* Collage elements (scrapbook paper, fibers, beads, tassels and mixed-media elements)
* Glitter
* Scissors
* Small paintbrush
* Glaze
* Craft glue

After making two dozen hard-boiled eggs one Easter, I looked at the big pile of eggshells on my counter and had a thought: How cute would tiny eggshell mosaics be?

This project is a wonderful way to showcase your family photographs, whether they are vintage photos or current ones. The eggshell mosaic is a unique way to complement the photo, and with four eggshell mosaics, the shadow box makes a perfect display. I have one displayed on the mantel, but they could be hung on a wall as well.

Using personal photos makes the project even more special. Vintage photos of parents and grandparents create a sentimental feel. Recent photos of your children, loved ones, or pets can preserve precious memories for years to come.

1 Prepare eggshells

To get clean eggshells, boil the eggs. After they are done, rinse them in a cold bath of water to make removing the shells easier. Crack each shell once and slip out the egg. Don't worry if the shell cracks into small pieces. Lay the eggshells on a paper towel or your work surface and let them dry thoroughly.

2 Paint eggshells

Paint the eggshells in assorted colors. You can add fine glitter to the shells while the paint is still wet for a lovely effect. Set the shells aside and let the paint dry.

3 Prepare matboard

Paint the outer edges of the four 3" × 4" (8cm × 10cm) matboard pieces with a color that either complements your eggshell colors or makes a nice contrast. It's not necessary to paint the interiors. Keep in mind that all four finished matboard pieces will be grouped together, so you want their colors to match.

4 Add design

Add another design element, such as stamps or stencils, to one of the small matboard frames to give it more texture, color and visual interest.

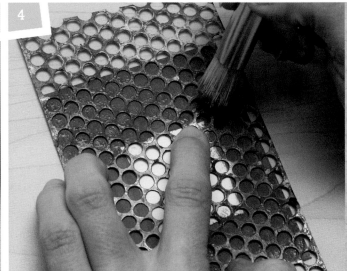

5

6

5 *Prepare photo*

Cut a piece of scrapbook paper and glue it in the center of the small matboard, then carefully cut out your photo to fit inside the scrapbook paper. Glue the photo to the scrapbook paper. Repeat steps 4 and 5 until all four of your photos are mounted.

6 *Lay mosaic*

Break the eggshells into various pieces small enough to easily fit around the photos. Glue the broken eggshell pieces around the edges of the photos. Make sure you leave space to show the scrapboook paper and painted backgrounds. Add other mixed-media elements to the frames if you like. Let the shells dry thoroughly. To give your eggshell mosaic extra protection, use a small paint-brush to apply a layer of clear glaze or lacquer.

7 *Add embellishment*

Turn each small frame over and add fibers, beads or tassels to the bottom of the frame, so the embellishment hangs below the edge.

8 *Assemble shadowbox*

Using your computer's word processor, type the word *FAMILY* in a font of your choosing, leaving plenty of space between the letters, and print it on a piece of cardstock. Cut out a square around each of the letters. Using leftover eggshells, create an eggshell mosaic border around each letter. Glue the letters in the middle of the 9" × 12" (23cm × 30cm) piece of matboard painted black. Glue two of the frames above the word and the other two below, spacing them evenly. Place the larger matboard in the shadow box.

7

8

tip MAKE A COPY of the original photograph and cut out the subject from the photographed background. Place this on the colorful, embellished matboard. This will really help the subject stand out!

What one loves

in childhood

stays in the

heart forever.
-Anonymous

Magical Memories

WHAT YOU'LL NEED

* 6" × 24" (15cm × 61cm) piece of MDF

* Four 3" × 4" (8cm × 10cm) pieces of ⅛" (3mm) glass

* ⅜" × ⅜" (10mm × 10mm) vitreous glass pieces in red, pink, orange and yellow

* 4" × 4" (10cm × 10cm) white tiles

* Eight small flat-backed colored glass marbles

* Acrylic paint in red, pink, orange, yellow and black

* Permanent black marker

* Computer and printer

* White printer paper

* Scissors

* Tile nippers

* Painter's tape

* White craft glue

* Tile adhesive

* Black grout

I love the power of the written word. It can bring meaning to our conscious and subconscious feelings, and when it's combined with visual art, it can provoke intense emotion. Poetry and quotes often are my inspiration for mosaics. This anonymous quote about celebrating childhood inspired me to use bright colors and simple shapes in this mosaic.

Placing the words under glass is an effective way to make the poetry or inspirational quote the focal point of the mosaic, and it gives the words a timeless quality.

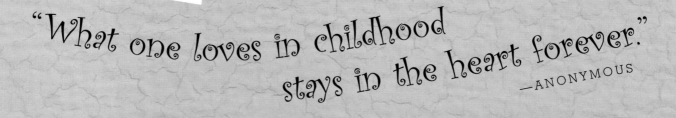

"What one loves in childhood stays in the heart forever."
—ANONYMOUS

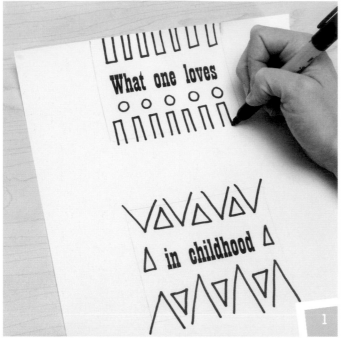

1   2

3   4

1 Print quote

Using a computer, printer and white paper, type, style and print out the inspirational poem or quote into four sections that will fit underneath the 3" × 4" (8cm × 10cm) pieces of glass. Draw simple, fun designs around the quotes, making sure the designs will also fit nicely beneath the glass.

2 Decorate designs

Use a brush and acrylic paint to decorate the designs. Cut out the quote and designs so they will fit beneath the glass.

3 Assemble board

Use white craft glue to glue the quotes under the rectangles of glass. Spread the glue on the glass, then press the paper with the quotes in place. Center the glass pieces with the quotes along the 6" × 24" (15cm × 61cm) board, then glue them in place.

4 Outline quotation

Use the small vitreous glass squares to outline the four pieces of glass.

5 *Lay background*
Place two flat-backed beads evenly between each of the glass-covered quotes, then fill the background with white tile using tile adhesive.

6 *Grout*
Once the adhesive is dry, tape off the glass and edges with painter's tape, then grout the background with black grout. Once dry, clean the grout. Remove the tape and paint the edges red.

Words to Live By

I especially enjoy finding quotes about art, or quotes from famous artists. This quote by Pablo Picasso is framed by mirrors cut into triangular shapes. The reflective surface of the mirror contrasts nicely with the bright pink grout.

You can create your own variation by finding a quote or poem that you've written, or using one that holds meaning to you.

"You must not ever stop

Bold and Brave

being whimsical."

— MARY OLIVER

Once you have a good grasp of basic mosaic techniques, it's time to expand your creative horizons even more. Using a jigsaw to shape your surfaces allows you the freedom to create any design you can imagine. You can design mosaics that are unique, exciting, whimsical and one-of-a-kind, and suddenly the impossible doesn't seem so impossible anymore!

As with any power tool, please use safety procedures, be aware of manufacturer's instructions and review the guidelines for using a jigsaw on page 16. But don't be afraid to explore new techniques in your mosaics. Not only will you be discovering a new tool and new possibilities, you'll be pushing yourself as well. Enjoy!

Forbidden Fruit

WHAT YOU'LL NEED

* 18" × 24" (46cm × 61cm) piece of MDF
* 4" × 4" (10cm × 10cm) dark green and light green ceramic tiles
* Brown stained glass
* Small ceramic apples (may be purchased in craft stores)
* Brown and dark green acrylic paint
* Jigsaw
* Paintbrush
* Pencil
* Tile nippers
* Glass cutter
* Safety goggles
* Painter's tape
* White craft glue
* Tile adhesive
* White grout
* Pattern (page 119)

Sometimes, an apple tree is more than just an apple tree.

Apples are a diverse source of symbolism. Throughout history, stories and myths are filled with magical apples. Many testify to the apple being the fruit of love, representing fertility, immortality and eternal youth. Probably the best-known story concerning apples occurs in the biblical tale of Adam and Eve. Apples are seen as magical, holding great promise but also danger. Even today, there is something both beautiful and powerful about apples that we respond to.

To me, the apple is a universal symbol of the giving and receiving of love, and a mosaic such as this would be a beautiful gift for someone you care for.

1 Prepare surface

Lay out the MDF panel and transfer the pattern from page 119 to the surface. Using your jigsaw, cut out the shape of the apple tree. (See page 16 for information and safety tips for using the jigsaw.) Sand the edges of the tree, draw the interior pattern, and then prime the surface with a 1:4 solution of craft glue and water.

2 Begin mosaic

Use your tile nippers to cut the dark green tile into small pieces. Follow the outline of the leaves with the dark green tiles, securing them with tile adhesive as you work.

3 Finish leaves

Space your apples evenly around the top of the tree and glue them down. Fill in the rest of the area of the leaves with light green tiles that have been nipped into small pieces.

4 Finish mosaic

Using the glass cutter, score and break the brown stained glass into strips and a variety of smaller mosaic shapes. Use the brown glass to fill in the bark of the tree. Let the adhesive dry overnight.

5   6

5 *Grout*

Cover the edge of the tree with painter's tape. Grout the tree with white grout. (See page 17 for more information on grout.) Once the grout has dried, clean the mosaic with an old towel.

6 *Paint*

After the grout has dried completely, remove the tape and paint the edges to match the tile. The top will be green, and the bottom edges will be painted brown.

More Than a Tree

You'll find this variation very different from the apple tree. It is abstract in nature, while the apple tree is symbolic. I used black tile to outline the shape of a tree with branches, and filled in the foliage with different leaves cut from cups, bowls and plates. I used a beautiful blue stained glass that is very reflective for the rain in the background, and chose a light green grout to highlight the many colors.

Mystical Mermaid

WHAT YOU'LL NEED

* 2' × 1' (61cm × 30cm) piece of MDF

* 4" × 4" (10cm × 10cm) yellow and flesh-colored ceramic tiles

* Tile or crockery to represent the mermaid fins

* Two matching shells

* Acrylic paint in the following colors: black, white, flesh, red, blue

* Pencil

* Tile nippers

* Jigsaw

* Safety goggles

* Cotton-tipped applicator

* Paintbrush

* Hook

* Hammer and nail

* Painter's tape

* Tile adhesive

* White craft glue

* White grout

* Pattern (page 120)

I was about nine years old

when I saw Darryl Hannah and Tom Hanks in the movie *Splash*. I still remember the magic of the mermaid in that movie. I've always seen the mermaid as an alluring symbol. As a native Floridian who spent every summer of my childhood at the beach, I felt mermaids personified the strength and power of the ocean.

An obsession with the mythical creatures has followed me into adulthood, and I love artwork and poetry that feature mermaids. The elusiveness of these human-like sea creatures has spawned my own series of mermaid artwork, including this fun and whimsical mixed-media mosaic.

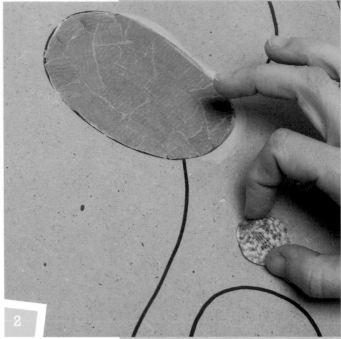

1 *Prepare surface*

Transfer the mermaid pattern on page 120 to the MDF. Cut out the shape with a jigsaw. (See page 16 for information on using a jigsaw.) Prepare the surface using a solution of craft glue and water (1:4). When dry, transfer the interior pattern and paint the face using flesh-colored acrylic paint.

2 *Add shells*

After the paint dries, carefully tape off the face with painter's tape. Glue down the seashells that will be the mermaid's bra.

3 *Begin mosaic*

Use tile nippers to nip the tiles. Glue the yellow tile down for the mermaid's flowing hair. Glue flesh-colored tile in the upper body, making sure to work around the shells.

tip IF YOU PAINT the seashells with polyacrylic sealer, they won't be so porous. This gives the shells even more protection from the grout.

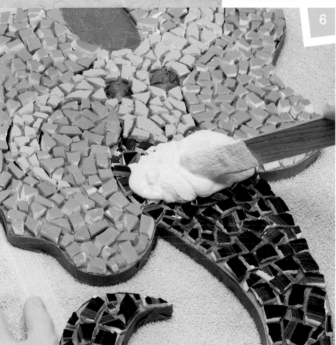

4 5

6

4 *Finish mosaic*
Cut the tile for the tail of the mermaid using triangular shapes when possible. This will create an illusion of fins in the mosaic. Glue the tile down for the tail.

5 *Apply tape*
Once the adhesive is dry, tape the sides of the mosaic using painter's tape, then tape over the shells, as they are porous and will absorb some of the grout.

6 *Grout*
Grout the mermaid using white grout. Make sure the grout penetrates all the spaces between the tesserae.

tip   THIS PROJECT LENDS ITSELF to many variations. Change the color of the hair or flesh of the mermaid, or use a real person as the inspiration for the face (though you should probably make sure the person doesn't mind being immortalized as a mermaid). Look for tile that gives the illusion of scales and fins. There are plenty of simple ways to really personalize this project.

tip

KEEP YOUR MERMAID SAFE! If you display her outside, make sure you
don't hang her where she will get wet, and bring her in when it gets cold.

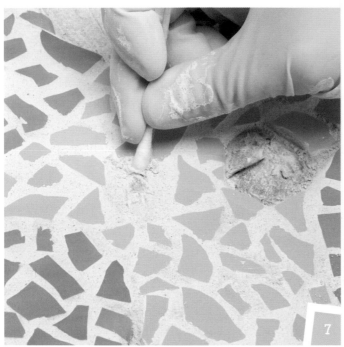

7 *Clean shells*
When dry, clean the grout from the mosaic.
To keep the grout from damaging the shells,
use a cotton-tipped applicator to clean
around them.

8 *Paint edges*
After the piece is completely dry, remove
the tape. Paint the edges of the mermaid
using white acrylic paint.

9 *Draw face*
Paint the mermaid's face with another coat
of flesh-colored acrylic paint. When the paint
is dry, use the pattern provided to add her
face—or draw it in freehand—using a pema-
nent ink marker.

10 | 11

10 *Paint face*

Paint her eyes and lips, then outline her features with black paint or a black permanent marker.

11 *Add hook*

Add a hook to the back of the mermaid. Create a hole for the hook with a hammer and nail. Make sure the mermaid is balanced when she hangs before securing the hook.

The Coy Geisha

This variation on the mermaid is another female figure I admire and enjoy using in my artwork. Geishas are professional female entertainers who perform traditional Japanese arts, such as the tea ceremony, dancing, singing, calligraphy, conversation and flower arrangement.

A successful geisha represents beauty, grace, charm, etiquette, refinement and artistic talent.

Glimpse into Mother Earth

WHAT YOU'LL NEED

* 38" × 18" (97cm × 46cm) piece of MDF
* River rocks
* Small pieces of mirror
* 4" × 4" (10cm × 10cm) ceramic tiles in the following colors: deep purple, mustard, cream and dark green
* Small ceramic leaves
* Flat-backed glass marbles in an orange or terra cotta color
* Acrylic paints in plum, cream, dark brown and terra cotta
* Crackle paint
* Paintbrush
* Jigsaw
* Pencil
* Tile nippers
* Gloves
* Safety goggles
* Eyescrews and wire
* Painter's tape
* Clear adhesive
* Tile adhesive
* Beige grout
* Pattern (page 121)

This series of panels is meant to represent the many layers of Mother Earth. It is inspired by a trip I took to the Grand Canyon a few years ago. Growing up on the East Coast and living near the ocean, I had no experience with mountains. The layers and colors in the Grand Canyon were fascinating. When I witnessed the breathtaking sight, I felt like I had gotten my first glimpse into Mother Earth.

The rippling curves of the panels, the earth-tone colors and the use of pebbles are symbolic of my impressions of the Grand Canyon. The shards of mirror and colored pebbles bring a subtle spirituality to the piece.

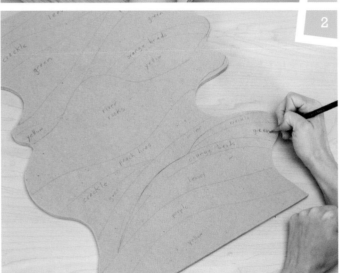

1 *Prepare surface*
Lay out MDF panel and transfer the pattern on page 121. Using your jigsaw, cut out each individual panel, making sure the edges match to maintain the illusion of a "puzzle." (See page 16 for more information on using the jigsaw.)

2 *Plan design*
Using the pattern as a guide, begin planning the mosaic. Plan what colors and tesserae will go in each section of the mosaic. Work on each panel individually, but try to keep each section of the mosaic consistent over the panels, so it would appear that each section moves across the panels.

3 *Paint surface*
Work on one panel at a time. Start by painting the middle sections, where the river rock will be, with purple acrylic paint. Next, paint the sections that will be crackled with cream acrylic paint. After the paint dries, crackle following the directions on the bottle. When dry, paint over the crackle with the dark brown acrylic paint. Finally, cover the paint with painter's tape once it has dried.

4 *Lay mosaic*
Carefully cut small pieces of mirror. Lay the mirror sections on the panel, securing the tesserae with tile adhesive. Fill in the ceramic leaf section, followed by the dark green pieces and mustard pieces cut into rectangles with your tile nipper. Glue down the glass beads next. As you finish laying the tesserae for one section, move to the next. Finish all three panels this way.

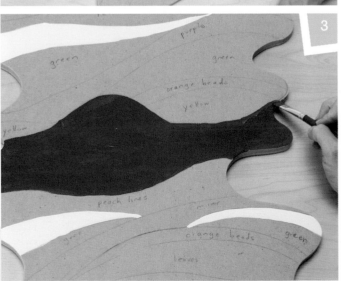

 tip WEAR SAFETY GOGGLES and gloves while cutting the mirror.

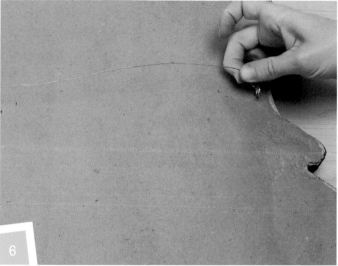

5 6

5 *Lay rock*

Cover the edges and the painted sections with tape. Carefully grout each individual section with tan grout. Do one section at a time to ensure that the grout doesn't dry too quickly, and that you clean up each section appropriately. (See page 17 for more information on grouting.) After the mosaic is clean and completely dry, remove the tape and fill in the purple sections with river rocks using a clear adhesive. Let the adhesive dry overnight.

6 *Add wire*

Paint the edges of the panel with terra cotta acrylic paint. Turn the panel over and add eyescrews and wire to hang. Finish the rest of the panels this way.

The Rainbow River

This variation is actually made on one piece of wood. The ripples are drawn and the spaces between panels are painted black. It flows like a river, and various shades of tile help evoke the beauty of a rainbow. The use of mirror adds a reflective texture to the piece.

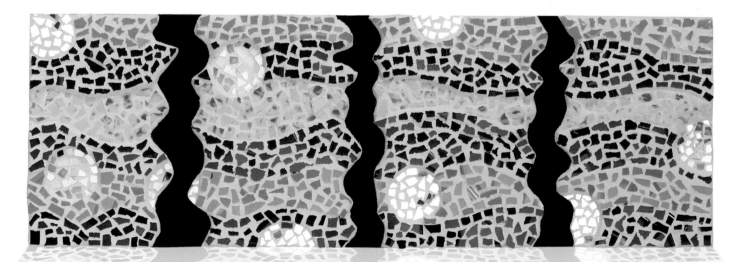

"Once you have tasted flight, you will forever walk the earth with your eyes turned skyward,

Taking It to the Exteme

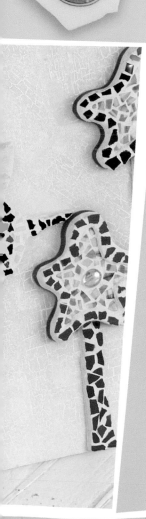

These projects take you beyond conventional mosaics. We leave behind working on flat surfaces and explore furniture and three-dimensional forms. You'll find lots of opportunities to personalize these projects and add your own creative and unique touch. You'll be using many skills you learned in previous projects—such as working with a jigsaw, using mixed media and creating inspirational pieces—but we're going to push the envelope and take it to the extreme.

These projects aren't necessarily any harder than the projects you've done before; they are just mosaics that have been designed "outside the box." They are meant to push you to explore what you can do with mosaics, to look at the possibilities from a new angle and see what you've done so far with fresh eyes. And, at the same time, these projects look mind-blowing! It is my hope and intention that by the end of this book, you will feel like a real mosaic artist who isn't afraid to try new things and can see the exciting results waiting for you when you take it to the extreme.

I strongly urge you to push your creative talents and always strive to try something new. I know you'll be happy where the journey will lead you.

Birds of Paradise

WHAT YOU'LL NEED

* Side table [this one is 20" (51cm) high, with a 12" × 12" (30cm × 30cm) table surface that's ¾" (19mm) deep]

* 4" × 4" (10cm × 10cm) ceramic tiles in white, black, green and brown

* Ceramic hearts in various colors

* Clay

* Glazes in blue, white, black and green

* Craft knife

* Access to a kiln

* Tile nippers

* Tile adhesive

* Silicon adhesive

* Beige grout

* Grout sealer (optional)

* Pattern (page 122)

This charming side table is perfect for the porch or a cozy corner of your home. I love to fill my home with live plants and flowers, and this side table is a great companion among them.

I love birds, and much of my work features them. This design was inspired by a postage stamp, and using clay, a local kiln and glazes helped personalize the project and ensure that the focal point was a unique piece of art. Don't be afraid to use your own mixed-media art as the focal point of your mosaics.

You have many options when it comes to choosing a side table. This side table has a removable backer board. The mosaic is applied to the backer board and then inserted into the iron frame. The project is based on this type of table; however, you can pick up a side table at a garage sale or thrift store and transfer the design directly onto the table surface.

1 2
3 4

1 Prepare pattern and clay

Roll out a piece of clay that's approximately 9" × 11" (23cm × 28cm). Transfer the pattern on page 122 onto the backer board of the table, then transfer the birds onto a piece of paper. Cut the birds from the paper and lay them on your clay. Cut out the birds from the clay using a craft knife. Let the clay birds dry for a few hours and use a wet sponge to smooth out any rough edges, then fire the birds in a kiln. They will need to be fired for eight hours.

2 Finish birds

After the clay is fired, decorate the birds with glazes. Afterward, the clay will need to be fired again. They will be shiny and non-porous after this process. Glue the birds to the middle of your backer board, using the pattern as a guide.

3 Begin mosaic

Start the mosaic by gluing down the black legs of the birds first. Glue the brown glass limb next, then the green leaves on the tree. Glue ceramic hearts around the birds, scattering them randomly in the background. You may want to plan where to place the hearts first, then secure them with glue.

4 Lay background

Use your nippers to cut white tiles out for the background. Glue the white tiles around the birds using tile adhesive. After all your tiles are glued down, let the mosaic dry overnight.

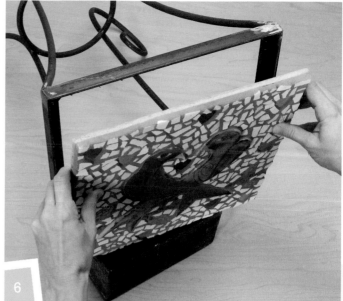

5 6

5 *Grout*

When the mosaic is finished, grout using tan grout. See page 17 for more information on using grout. Once the grout is dry, clean the mosaic using an old towel. Make sure the ceramic hearts can be seen through the grout and the grout doesn't cover the edges of the hearts. If it does, you may need to pick away the grout.

6 *Assemble table*

Use silicon adhesive to glue your backer board down into the base of the table. If you plan to place the table outside, seal the grout with grout sealer.

tip

THIS PROJECT USES a clay piece made at a local ceramic shop that offers a kiln. If you don't have access to a kiln, search your local craft store for another suitable piece to use as a focal point for this mosaic, or draw the birds and fill them in with tile.

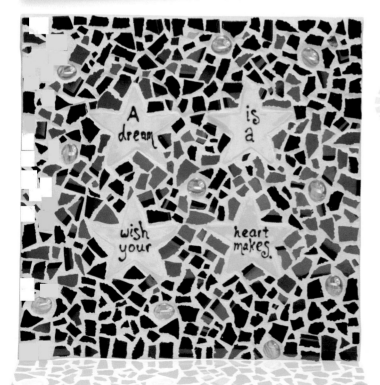

Celestial Wishes

If you have access to a kiln, you can create just about anything you want out of clay and incorporate it into a mosaic. In this variation, after rolling out the clay, cookie cutters were used to cut out the stars and glaze was used to write the words. You can purchase glaze in small bottles with writing tips to create words on your clay pieces.

Using handmade clay pieces in your mixed-media mosaics makes them even more unique.

Rainy Days

WHAT YOU'LL NEED

* Dresser [this one is 21" (53cm) high, with a top surface of 14" × 18" (36cm × 46cm)]

* $1\frac{1}{2}$" × $\frac{5}{8}$" (4cm × 2cm) ceramic pieces in lime, light blue and white

* $\frac{3}{4}$" × $\frac{3}{4}$" (19mm × 19mm) vitreous tile squares in an assortment of pinks and purples

* $\frac{3}{4}$" × $\frac{3}{4}$" (19mm × 19mm) vitreous tile squares in an assortment of turquoise and blues

* 4" × 4" (10cm × 10cm) ceramic tiles in lavender and lime

* 5" × 7" (13cm × 18cm) piece of $\frac{1}{8}$" (3mm) glass

* Spray paint in pink, lavender and sage green

* Watercolors, colored pencils, markers and/or crayons (for decorating the picture)

* White paper

* Ruler

* Pencil

* Permanent ink marker

* Tile nippers

* Painter's tape

* Clear craft glue

* Tile adhesive

* White grout

* Pattern (page 123)

This charming little bedside dresser is perfect for a little girl or a grown woman who is a child at heart. The template provided depicts an adorable little girl protecting her tiny friends from a rainy day.

I found this nightstand at an antiques store. The owner thinks it was probably used as a sewing chest, but to me it looked like the perfect size for a little girl to store her treasures. Refurbishing or remaking furniture is a pleasure, and I always love to add a little mixed-media mosaic to the finished piece.

The picture is definitely the focal point of this project, while the mosaic makes a wonderful frame. Have fun working on the picure! To create the texture in the rain clouds, I sprinkled a little salt on the watercolors while they were still wet. Explore your own creative touches with this project.

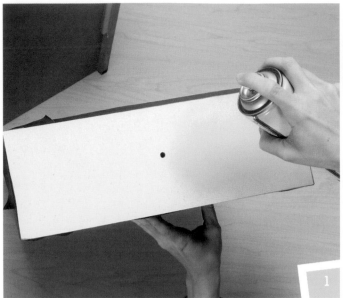

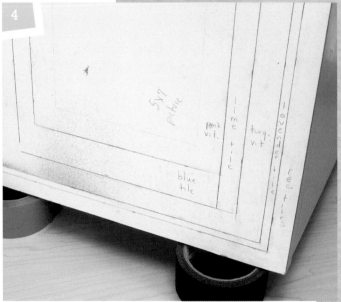

| 1 | 2 |
| 3 | 4 |

1 *Prepare surface*

Prepare the top surface of the dresser by sanding it lightly. Mix a solution of craft glue and water (1:4) and apply it to the surface. Tape off the edges of the drawers and the outside of the dresser. Paint the dresser. I used pink spray paint on two of the drawers, sage green on the rest, and lavender on the dresser. Remove the tape once the paint is dry.

2 *Decorate drawers*

Decorate the front of the drawers using acrylic paint and a permanent ink pen. Sketch out the designs first with a pencil. I used a variety of other simple shapes, such as hearts, circles and butterflies.

3 *Prepare picture*

Trace the template on a 5" × 7" (13cm × 18cm) piece of white paper. Use watercolors, colored pencils, markers and/or crayons to decorate the template. Make a color copy of the finished template. Spread a thin, even layer of white craft glue on the glass, and lay it on top of the color copy. Make sure the glue you use will dry clear.

4 *Prepare design*

After the glue is dry, place the picture in the middle of the dresser. Plan your mosaic using a pencil and ruler. Create borders around the picture. Outline the edge of the picture with your assortment of pink and purple vitreous tiles. Use a ruler to draw a 1'' border around the vitreous tiles. Fill other layers on the dresser with lime tiles.

5 *Begin mosaic*

Begin laying the mosaic. Go around the lime border with your assortment of turquoise and blue vitreous tiles. Continue the mosaic, making adjustments, if necessary, to the pattern as you work.

6 *Grout*

Let the dresser dry overnight. Carefully apply your white grout to the mosaic, protecting the glass with painter's tape. (See page 17 for more information on grouting.) Make sure there are no sharp edges in the mosaic before giving it to a young person! Replace the drawers once the grout is clean.

tip AS YOU PLAN the mosaic on top of the dresser, lay, but don't secure, tiles around the picture to see what you like. Try different combinations and varieties of tile before deciding on the layout.

Radical Robot

This variation is for a special little boy in your life. My sons love robots, and when I created this drawing I used two elements of collage to make the robot a little funkier: the eyes and the arms. Collage is a fun and easy way to create uniqueness and originality in your art.

When creating a boy's version of the dresser, use more masculine-colored tiles, such as black and silver.

The Queen Bee

WHAT YOU'LL NEED

* 19" × 25" (48cm × 64cm) piece of MDF
* 11" × 24" (28cm × 61cm) piece of MDF
* 4" × 4" (10cm × 10cm) ceramic tiles in black, yellow, dark green, white, brown, purple and pink
* Floral crockery with shades of pink and purple
* Brown crockery
* Five small gold flat-backed glass marbles
* Eight large clear flat-backed glass marbles
* Gold leaf tiles
* Artist pastels
* Blue stained glass
* Acrylic paint in the following colors: flesh, black, blue, red, purple, pink, beige and white
* Crackle paint
* Computer and printer
* Jigsaw
* Safety goggles
* Painter's tape
* Tile nippers
* Clear craft glue
* Tile adhesive
* White grout
* Polyacrylic sealant
* Pattern (page 124)

A mosaic like this demands to be noticed. In mosaics, painted and crackled elements, grout, dimensional pieces and beautiful tile combine with stunning results. The variety of textures really helps the art stand out.

Although this project is more advanced and time-consuming than the previous ones, the results show. The three-dimensional aspect creates a depth and texture that is very appealing. For me, the queen bee represents my role in the household. Although she's in charge, she still needs flowers and pollen, as well as all the other bees to make things work.

The crackle paint and various uses of tesserae add to this project's mixed-media glory.

1 | 2
3 | 4

1 Transfer pattern

Prepare the surface of the larger MDF panel with a 1:4 solution of white craft glue and water. When dry, center the pattern on page 124 on the panel. Make adjustments as necessary to the position of elements in the pattern, then transfer the pattern lightly with a pencil to the surface.

2 Prepare flowers and bee

Copy the queen bee and flowers from the pattern on page 124 onto the smaller MDF panel. Carefully cut out the images using a jigsaw, then sand. (See page 16 for more information on using a jigsaw.) Prepare the wood with a 1:4 solution of white craft glue and water. Transfer the details of the pattern to the MDF.

3 Assemble flowers

Starting with one of the flowers, outline the outer edge with purple or pink tile. Center a gold marble in the middle of the flower and fill in the rest with your floral crockery. Finish all five flowers this way.

4 Paint face

Paint the face of the bee with flesh-colored acrylic paint. After the paint dries, tape it off with painter's tape. The painted details of the face will be added when the bee is grouted.

5 *Begin the bee*

Use the tile nippers to nip the tiles for the bee into small pieces. Fill in her crown with gold tile, and her hair with brown crockery. Use black and yellow tile to fill the stripes on her body. Use white tile for the wings.

6 *Finish the bee*

Finish the mosaic on the bee. Make sure the mosaic is complete and there are no bare spots, especially around the face. Let the adhesive dry overnight.

7 *Basecoat*

Basecoat the panel with white paint, painting around the areas on the panel that have a mixed-media piece over them. Let the paint dry.

8 *Assemble letters*

As the paint dries, use your computer's word processor to type and print out the words *QUEEN BEE* in the font of your choice, leaving plenty of space between the letters. Using a small amount of white craft glue, glue one large clear flat-backed glass marble on top of each letter. When dry, cut out the letters and glass marbles from the paper.

5 6

7 8

9 *Paint arms and basket*

Draw in the arms and the basket on the panel using a pencil, then paint them using acrylic paint. Make sure the arms are long enough that they appear natural beneath the mixed-media body.

10 *Crackle background*

Following the directions on your bottle, paint your white background in sections with crackle paint. Let the crackle paint sit for approximately 10 minutes, then paint over the crackle with a light blue acrylic paint. It should begin crackling momentarily. Do not paint layers over the crackle, or it will disturb the natural pattern. When the crackle is dry, use a white pastel to lightly mark where the sections are divided, then seal the surface with poly-acrylic sealant.

11 *Begin mosaic*

Place each of the wooden flowers on the surface and plan the flower stems. You may need to make adjustments to the position of the stems, depending on the position of the flowers. Use green broken tile to create the stems for each of the flowers. Glue the letters at the top of the panel, staggering them across the top. Glue tiny purple and pink pieces of tile around each of the letters.

tip LAY THE MIXED-MEDIA ELEMENTS, such as the flowers and queen bee, on the surface before you begin laying the mosaic pieces. Mark the position of the flowers. You may need to lay the mosaic pieces around them. Make sure to follow these guidelines carefully, as it will make assembling the mosaic easier.

tip · IF THE MIXED-MEDIA ELEMENTS feel too tight, try angling the pieces on the surface to find the perfect position. Continue to adjust the position of the elements until you are pleased with the layout before you begin gluing them down.

12 *Grout*

Apply painter's tape along the edges of the stems and around the tile that surrounds the letters. Use white grout on the bee and the flowers, as well as the stems and the tile around the letters. Grout the queen bee and flower mixed-media elements as well. (For more information on grouting, see page 17.) Once the grout is dry, clean it from the mosaic.

13 *Finish the bee and flowers*

Remove the tape from the surface, bee and flowers. Paint the edges of the flowers in purple and pink acrylic paint. Finish painting the details on the bee. Lightly apply a stroke of beige acrylic paint to the brown tile in her hair to add texture, then paint the edges of the bee and the panel white.

14 *Finish mosaic*

Glue the bee on the surface so it appears her hands are attached to her body. Glue the flowers above each of the stems.

12

13 14

Fairy Amour

WHAT YOU'LL NEED

* 18" × 36" (46cm × 91cm) piece of MDF

* Orange, red and yellow flat pebble tiles (sold in craft stores)

* Glass "squiggles" embellishments

* 4" × 4" (10cm × 10cm) tiles in black, white, denim blue, black with yellow dots, and yellow

* Crockery with a flower pattern

* Gold tiles

* Mixed media elements such as game letters to spell *LOVE* and *HOPE*, and various jewelry, ceramic and crockery pieces

* Acrylic paints in the following colors: flesh, red, pink, copper, light blue, cobalt blue, black and yellow

* Jigsaw

* Black permanent marker

* Tile nippers

* Painter's tape

* Craft glue

* Tile adhesive

* White grout

* Pattern (page 125)

I incorporated a wealth of mixed-media elements in this project: painting, as well as mosaics that incorporate tile, glass, jewelry, crockery and game letters.

I feel a great emotional attachment to this fairy of love. The wings represent freedom and the possibility that anything can happen. The jewelry pieces in the mosaic were family items from my mother. The fairy is holding a heart that says, "Listen to Your Heart." She is my interpretation of feminine love that represents the roles in my life as mother, wife, daughter and friend.

Adding a personal touch to your mosaics makes them even more special. Use your mosaics to both reflect and explore who you are.

1 *Prepare surface*

Transfer the pattern on page 125 to the MDF panel. Cut out the pattern using a jigsaw and following the directions on page 16. Sand the edges, then prepare the surface with a solution of 1:4 craft glue and water. When dry, draw the interior of the pattern on the MDF. Go over the lines of the pattern using a permanent ink pen.

2 *Paint fairy*

Paint the hands, heart, feet and face of the fairy using flesh-colored acrylic paint. Once the paint is dry, protect the painted areas with painter's tape.

3 *Begin mosaic*

Outline the panel using the flat yellow, orange and red pebble tiles.

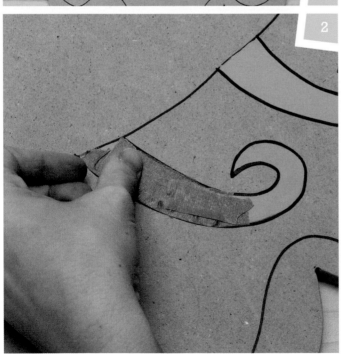

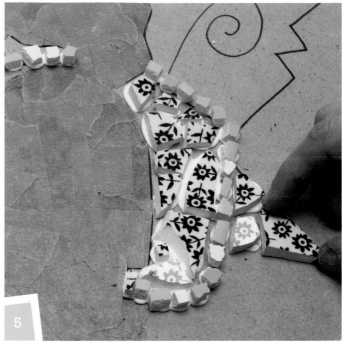

4 5

6

4 *Add border*

Using a ruler, measure off the sides into seven 3" (8cm) squares. Lay out glass squiggle tesserae in each square, then fill the rest of the squares with alternating black and white tile nipped into small pieces.

5 *Add dress*

Outline the fairy's dress using small pieces of nipped yellow tile. fill the inside of the dress using broken flowered crockery pieces. The crockery should be larger than the tile.

6 *Add crown*

Fill the crown with gold tile nipped into small pieces. Shape the gold tile using the tile nippers to make the crown seem fuller.

tip FINDING MIXED-MEDIA ELEMENTS is fun. I look for jewelry, buttons, shells, game piece letters and any other random objects that add interest and color to my mosaics. Garage sales, thrift shops and flea markets are good places to look for mixed-media elements. Almost anything goes. The only thing you need to keep in mind is that some porous mixed-media pieces will absorb the grout. Anything porous should be either sealed or taped off before grouting. Fragile mixed-media pieces should be glued on after the mosaic has been grouted.

7 *Nip tile*

Continue the mosaic. First, place the mixed-media elements and black and yellow tile circles in the background, planning the area around the fairy. Cut blue tile into pieces larger than the other tile or crockery elements to fill in the background.

8 *Add background*

Next, begin laying the blue tile background around the mixed-media elements and complete the rest of the mosaic, such as the wings, the circles of black and yellow tile and the white tile sides of the mosaic.

9 *Grout*

When you've completed the mosaic, cover the mixed-media elements with painter's tape. Mix white grout with light blue acrylic paint to make light blue grout, then grout the mosaic. When dry, clean off the grout and clear the tiles with an old towel.

10 *Add mixed-media elements*

Remove the painter's tape. Check the mixed-media elements, making sure they're still secure. If necessary, glue them in place again.

11 *Finish painting*

Paint another basecoat on the face, neck, hands and heart first, then add other details such as lips, eyes and swirls in the hair. Outline the features with black paint, then drybrush pink on the heart. Finish with the words on the heart. Let the paint dry between layers.

12 *Paint edges*

Finish the edges of the mosaic with yellow paint.

tip

IF YOU'RE WORRIED about a delicate mixed-media piece surviving the grout and mosaic process, just glue it in place after you're finished. While you're working, use a larger and less delicate piece to hold its place in the mosaic.

She Danced until the Sun Came Up

Dancing has always been a passion of mine, and this woman represents the youthfulness, vigor and fun that is embodied in dancing.

The words are typed and glued under clear, flat-backed glass marbles. I used scrapbook paper under glass for the flower petals, and stained glass for the sun.

Patterns

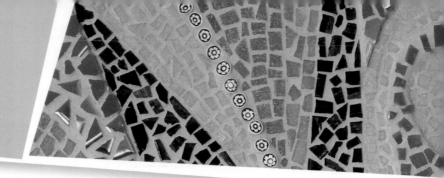

The Night Cat, page 24.
Enlarge this pattern at 122%
to bring to full size.

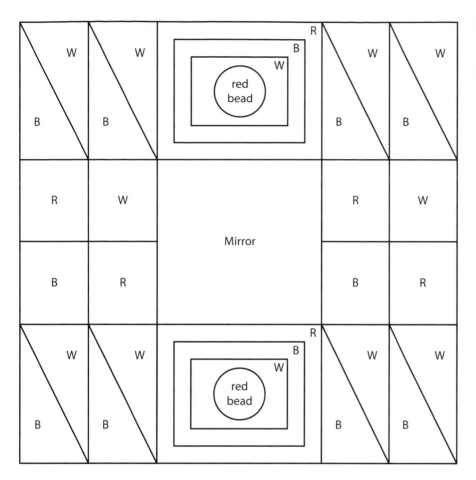

Do You See What I See?, page 38. Enlarge this pattern at 175% to bring to full size.

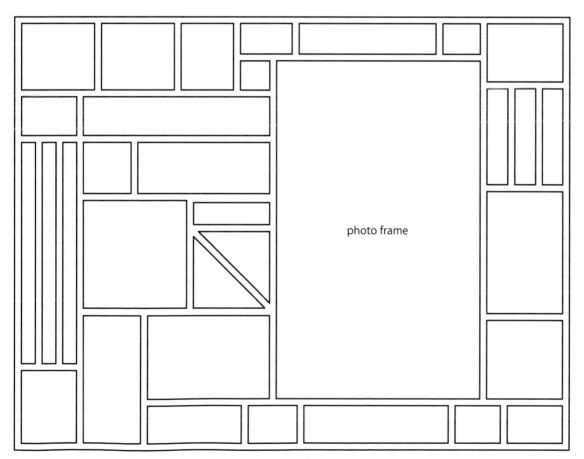

Textured Tiles, page 46. Enlarge this pattern at 175% to bring to full size.

mirror

Golden Visions, page 54.
Enlarge this pattern at 200%.
Then enlarge again at 121% to
bring to full size.

Bloom, page 60. Enlarge this pattern at
167% to bring to full size.

Truth Is Universal, page 64.

Forbidden Fruit, page 78.

Mystical Mermaid, page 82. Enlarge this pattern at
200%. Then enlarge again at 111% to bring to full size.

Glimpse into Mother Earth, page 88. Enlarge this pattern at 200%. Then enlarge again at 175% to bring to full size.

Birds of Paradise, page 94.
Enlarge this pattern at 119%
to bring to full size.

Rainy Days, page 98. Enlarge this pattern at
122% to bring to full size.

The Queen Bee, page 102. Enlarge this pattern at 200%.
Then enlarge again at 128% to bring to full size.

Fairy Amour, page 108. Enlarge this pattern first at
200%. Then enlarge again at 200%. Then enlarge
again at 130% to bring to full size.

Resources

Tools, supplies and tesserae for mosaic projects are available at your local craft and hobby stores, as well as at nurseries, garden centers, stained glass and home inprovement centers. Look in your local phone book for stores near you. Below are a few other resources you might find useful.

Art Glass Association
www.artglassassociation.com
Association of glass artists, retailers, suppliers and hobbyists

Delphi
800-248-2048
www.delphiglass.com
Ceramic tile, smalti and pre-cut stained glass tesserae

Delta Technical Coating, Inc.
800-423-4135
www.deltacrafts.com
Rubber stamps, paints and other mixed-media mosaic products

Mosaic Mercantile
877-9-MOSAIC
www.mosaicmercantile.com
Mosaic tile, kits and accessories

Plaid Enterprises, Inc.
800-842-4197
www.plaidonline.com
Grout, tile nippers, kits, mosaic adhesives and more

Rupert, Gibbon & Spider, Inc.
800-442-0455
www.jacquardproducts.com
Jacquard Lumiere metallic and pearlescent colors

Society of American Mosaic Artists
www.americanmosaics.org
Nonprofit society of mosaic art and artists with online links to workshops and classes

Tile Heritage Foundation
www.tileheritage.org
Nonprofit organization dedicated to the appreciation and preservation of ceramic surfaces in America

Weldbond
800-388-2001
www.weldbondusa.com
Mosaic adhesive

WitsEnd Mosaic
888-4-WITS-END
www.WitsEndMosaic.com
Online resource for mosaic artists, offering both supplies and instruction

For further inspiration, check out the work of the following mosaic artists:

Steve Terlizzese (www.mosaicguy.com)
Laurie Mika (www.mikaarts.com)
Irina Charny (www.icmosaics.com)
Laurel True (www.truemosaics.com)
Sonia King (www.mosaicworks.com)

Index

A

A Chorus of Light, 23
A Creative Concoction, 45
acrylic paints, 13
adhesives, 11, 12, 13
apple tree mosaic, 78–81, 119

B

Birds of Paradise, 94–97, 122
Bloom, 60–63, 117
bottles, 21, 23

C

candle holders, 20–23
cat mosaic, 24–27, 114
Celestial Wishes, 97
ceramic tile, 10, 14
Chinese symbols, 64–67
clay. *See* polymer clay
collage, 45, 101
colors, 13, 35, 49, 61, 70
crockery, 10

D

Do You See What I See?, 38–41, 115
dresser project, 98–101

E

Eclectic Clutch, 32–35
embellishments, 25, 27, 49, 70, 71

F

Fairy Amour, 108–113, 125
flower vases, 28–31, 60–63
Forbidden Fruit, 78–81, 119
frames, 37, 43–45, 46–49, 68–71
furniture, 11, 94–97, 98–101

G

glass, 10, 11
    bottles, 21, 23
    scoring, 15
glass cutters, 12
Glimpse into Mother Earth, 88–91, 121
Golden Visions, 54–57, 116
graphite, 11

grout, 13, 111
    cleaning off, 31
    coloring, 13
    mixing, 12, 17
    using, 17

I

inspiration, 57, 59, 73

J

jigsaws, 16, 52, 56, 77

K

kilns, 97

M

Magical Memories, 72–75
Majestic Roses, 50–53
materials, 10
    eggshells, 69–71
    marbles, 39–40, 43–44, 110
    mixed-media elements, 10, 111, 113
    pebbles, 89, 91, 110
    seashells, 41, 83–86
medium-density fiberboard (MDF), 11
mirrors, 37
    with geometric shapes, 38–41
    "Klimt" style, 54–57
    with roses, 50–53
    scoring, 15
    with seashells, 41
More than a Tree, 81
Mother Earth, 88–91, 121
Music Heals the Soul, 63
Mystical Mermaid, 82–87, 120

N

Night Cat, 24–27
nipping tile, 12, 14

O

owl, 27

P

paints, 13
paper, 10, 63

patterns
    Birds of Paradise, 122
    cat, 114
    Fairy Amour, 125
    flower vases, 117
    frames, 115, 116
    mermaid, 120
    Mother Earth, 121
    Queen Bee, 124
    Rainy Days, 123
    transferring, 11
    tree, 119
    truth symbol, 118
Perfect Balance, 67
photographs. *See* picture frames
picture frames, 37, 42–45, 46–49, 68–71
pique assiette, 45
polymer clay, 10, 47, 48, 49
    colors, 61
    cutting, 63
    sealers, 13
purse, 32–35

Q

Queen Bee, 103–107, 124
quotes, 73–75, 97, 109, 113

R

Radical Robot, 101
Rainy Days, 98–101, 123
roses, 51

S

safety precautions, 12, 15, 16, 90
Sea Yourself, 41
sealers, 12, 13, 84, 111
Seeds of Sunshine, 53
Sentimental Elements, 68–71
shadowbox project, 68–71
She Danced Until the Sun Came Up, 113
smalti, 10
stained glass, 15, 81
sunflowers, 53
supplies, 12–13
surfaces, 11
Swirls and Glass, 28–31

T

table surface mosaic, 94–97
techniques
    assembling mosaics, 106
    layouts, 101, 106, 107
    nipping tile, 14
    scoring glass, 15
    using grout, 17
    using jigsaws, 16
tesserae, 10
    breaking, 12
    coffee mugs, 27
    flowers, 51, 53
    small pieces, 30
Textured Tiles, 46–49, 115
The Coy Geisha, 87
The Night Cat, 24–27, 114
The Queen Bee, 103–107, 124
The Rainbow River, 91
three-dimensional projects, 93, 102–107
tile, 10
    embellishing, 49
    nipping, 14
tile nippers, 12, 14
tools, 12–13, 16
Truth is Universal, 64–67, 118

V

vases, 29–31, 60–63
vitreous glass, 10
    cleaning, 31

W

Whooo Are You?, 27
wine bottle candle holders, 20–23
wood, 11, 33
Words to Live By, 75

Y

yin and yang pattern, 67
You Are My Sunshine, 42–45

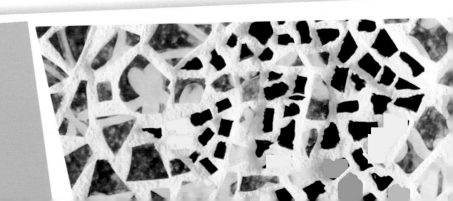

Be Inspired with North Light Books!

Garden Mosaics Made Easy

By Cliff Kennedy & Jane Wendling Pompilio
Mosaics are a simple, elegant way to enhance the natural beauty of your home and garden. Jane Pompilio and Cliff Kennedy will show you how to add the subtle charm of mosaics through 25 step-by-step mosaic projects featuring ready-to-use design templates. You'll learn how to create projects based on a photograph, or incorporate memory art in your mosaics. You'll find a wealth of tips on using a wide variety of creative materials such as stained glass, china, pottery, shells and more, as well as a quick primer on contemporary mosaic techniques such as groutless mosaics and direct and indirect methods of laying tile. Gardening enthusiasts and crafters alike will find a book bursting with ideas and inspirations!
ISBN-10: 1-58180-720-1
ISBN-13 978-1-58180-720-2
Paperback 128 pages 33393

Easy Mosaics for Home and Garden

By Sarah Donnelly
Create a range of stylish and clever mosaics using the simple "embedded" technique detailed inside. You'll find 20 appealing projects, from garden stepping stones and table tops to paper weights, sundials and more. Each one comes complete with step-by-step instructions, materials lists and templates you can enlarge and trace. There's no tile to cut, no messy grout to deal with. Just pick a project and get creative!
ISBN-10: 1-58180-129-7
ISBN- 13 978-1-58180-129-3
paperback 128 pages 31830

Collage Unleashed

By Traci Bautista
Learn to collage using everything but the kitchen sink with this bright and playful book. Author Traci Bautista show you there are no mistakes in making art. You can combine anything—from paper, fabric, paint and even paper towels to beads, metal, doodles and stitching to create unique art books, fabric journals and mixed media paintings. The book includes detailed instructions for lots of innovative techniques, such as staining/dying paper towels, freestyle hand lettering, doodling, funky embroidery and crayon transfers. Then you'll learn how to turn your new-found techniques into dazzling projects.
ISBN-10: 1-58180-845-3
ISBN-13 978-1-58180-845-2
paperback 128 pages Z0024

These and other fine North Light titles are available from your local art and craft retailer, bookstore or online supplier.